D0088645

UNIQUE EATS AND EATERIES

OF

SEATTLE

Copyright © 2018, Reedy Press, LLC
All rights reserved.
Reedy Press
PO Box 5131
St. Louis, MO 63139
www.reedypress.com

No part of this publication may be reproduced or transmitted in any form or by any means, electronic or mechanical, including photocopy, recording, or any information storage and retrieval system, without permission in writing from the publisher. Permissions may be sought directly from Reedy Press at the above mailing address or via our website at www.reedypress.com.

Library of Congress Control Number: 2018945693
ISBN: 9781681061818

Book Design: Barbara Northcott

Printed in the United States of America
18 19 20 21 22   5 4 3 2 1

UNIQUE EATS AND EATERIES

OF

SEATTLE

JAKE UITTI

CONTENTS

INTRODUCTION

A few things define Seattle culture more than anything else—independent music, craft beer, nature, tech, and, of course, restaurants. The latter—dining—is the one that just about everyone in the city can agree upon to be quite important. We all gotta eat, after all, and ever since moving to the city eleven years ago from the East Coast, the Emerald City has fed me well and taught me much about cuisine.

I learned about pho in Seattle, about authentic ramen, about Dick's delicious burgers, about homemade tajarin noodles, and about the best drinks to wash these exquisite meals down. Seattle food culture is one of the most elaborate, refined, and exciting in the United States, and this book is my ode to that truth.

Within these pages, you'll hear directly from ninety of the city's top food authorities—many of them chef/owners—about the origins of their establishments and their menu philosophies. While we couldn't fit everyone or every place into this book, we think it is a great encapsulation of what's happening in the city right now. I hope it helps you fall in love with Seattle just as it made my heart melt like so much delicious mozzarella.

— Jake Uitti

UNIQUE EATS AND EATERIES

OF

SEATTLE

CAN CAN
CULINARY CABARET

You've likely seen pictures of fish flying in Seattle's downtown Pike Place Market. They are, after all, indelible images—some giant tuna tossed between two market workers wearing galoshes and rubber aprons—and they're often shown when a national publication or television outlet wants to display the goofy grandeur that is the historic downtown farmers market. But, as with most things, there is more than meets the eye to this well-trodden arena. Nestled below in what feels like the hull of the market is the subterranean Can Can Culinary Cabaret—what some lovingly refer to as Seattle's aphrodisiac—a dinner theater and restaurant like no other, offering an array of savory menu options paired with a barrage of professional burlesque dance moves.

Founded in 2005 by Can Can's owner, Chris Pink, an electric fellow with a pomp haircut and ambitions to grow his charming theater each season, the intimate, speakeasy locale offers just sixty seats to its hungry patrons. When the curtain goes up and the evening's host, Jonathan Bechtel (aka Johnny), steps onto the catwalk to greet the crowd, it's clear that something special is about to happen over dinner. "Ladies and gentlemen, welcome to the CAAAAANN CAAAAANN!" growls the boyishly handsome host, as forks clink on plates and glasses are raised to lips.

But Can Can, of course, is also a top-notch, satisfying restaurant offering such appetizers as Dungeness crab beignets with a Cajun remoulade or tenderloin poutine with locally produced Beecher's cheese curds melted overtop. Can Can also offers entrées, such as wild mushroom ravioli in a white cream sauce and seafood gumbo

Owner Chris Pink's number one priority when you visit Can Can is to entertain and satisfy. So much so, he'll even do jumping jacks in sandals for you!

with fried okra, all made by the loving hands of the house chef, who, between plates, might just show up during a Can Can number in a yellow polka dot bikini.

Residing in the heart of one of the world's most beloved markets has its benefits. Can Can is not shy about using ingredients sourced from shops above ground, whether that be the cheese curds or the butternut squash and caramelized onions used in the vegetarian, yet still quite decadent, butternut squash ravioli, topped with Parmesan cheese and a drizzled balsamic reduction, or even the dried rose buds floating in its signature cocktails.

Indeed, Can Can has all the ingredients to make up a memorable evening, whether for a bachelorette party or a special date night when you want to show your partner you know a little bit more about the historic Pike Place Market than do those who just come for the flying fish.

94 Pike St.
(206) 652-0832
thecancan.com

KONA KITCHEN

Where are they now? is a regular theme for glossy magazines and internet gossip websites to remember the actors we all loved from yesterday, with those memorable faces we grew up with in movies and television series but who have since left our lives for more pedestrian endeavors—faces like the one that belongs to Yuji Okumoto, otherwise known as the intimidating villain Chozen Toguchi in *The Karate Kid Part II*. In 2002, Yuji, who moved to Seattle from California to marry his wife after taking a step back from Hollywood, opened the Emerald City restaurant Kona Kitchen, a beloved hole-in-the wall spot serving some of the city's most delectable fried rice and loco mocos.

"When he moved up here, there wasn't much acting or production work," says his wife, Angela, who is from Washington. "So Yuji wanted to do something creative. He wanted to open a restaurant," and so the couple did. Walking into Kona Kitchen, you immediately feel a distinct neighborhood hangout vibe. There might be a family with young children savoring a bowl of wonton soup at one of the long corner tables, or there might be a gaggle of construction workers in their orange T-shirts and neon yellow suspenders devouring teriyaki burgers with pineapple slices or piping hot plates of fried chicken katsu.

Kona Kitchen, located in Seattle's Maple Leaf neighborhood, is representative of a larger theme in the Emerald City. The Census Bureau estimates that some forty-six thousand native Hawaiians or Pacific Islanders live in Washington State, many of whom reside

Try not to be star struck by all the Hollywood photos and autographs hanging from the walls of Kona Kitchen. It is, after all, co-owned by a former 80s star.

Nothing quite like sticky Hawaiian fried rice topped with a fried egg or two. And no one does that better than Kona Kitchen.

in Seattle. As a result, there is a hunger for the fare of the island homeland, and Kona Kitchen provides satiety for it with a menu supplemented by some traditional Japanese cuisine as well. Standout items include fried rice loco moco topped with a hamburger patty or chicken katsyu a fried egg, and brown gravy; waimea, a combination of thinly sliced teri beef and pork katsu; and saimin, a soup composed of noodles in broth topped with delicious barbecue pork.

Indeed, the quaint neighborhood kitchen is a home away from home for many. What it lacks in pretention and gaudiness it gains in relaxation and comfort food. If you're lucky, you might see Yuji hanging out with friends or working the counter with a smile. If so, you'll know there's no need to consult the glossy magazines. Instead, all you need to do is peruse the menu to order. You'll soon feel at home, happy, and yes, well fed.

8501 Fifth Ave. NE
(206) 517-5662
konakitchen.com

THE STATION

It was flirt at first sight, but little did they know what was about to happen, what would soon be born from a batted lash and a charming smile. Leona and Luis Rodriguez met as students at Nathan Hale High School in Seattle's north end. Leona, enrolled in a childhood psychology course, came around a corner one afternoon carrying a lifelike baby doll. "Is that your baby?" asked Luis. "You want to be the dad?" Leona playfully shot back, and now the couple, married with two young sons, owns and operates one of the hippest and certainly the most socially conscious cafés in the coffee-loving city.

The Station, located in Seattle's vibrant and diverse South End neighborhood, Beacon Hill, has offered artful lattes and its signature spicy Mexican Mocha since 2010. It welcomes people of all backgrounds, and don't be surprised if you're told to straighten up if you step out of the proverbial line. It's a hub for political activism, protest, and rich cultural collaboration. It's also the center of one of the city's most anticipated music festivals each year, Block Party at the Station, featuring talented artists who might not otherwise see a city main stage.

"I want everybody to come into the Station," says Leona. "I knew from the get-go it was going to be different from any other coffee shop. Luis opening a coffee shop was not going to be a Starbucks-type environment. We already know your name before you come in. We have your coffee ready by the time you go and order it."

In 2017, the Station moved from its smaller, well-worn location across the street to the Roberto Maestas Plaza, a place Luis says is a "non-gentrified building with a lot of our POC [people of color] friends." Indeed, diversity is celebrated at the Station, and while there are other eateries in the city to visit if you're in search of a fabulous three-course meal, the Station is the place where you can savor a cup

Come into the Station in the morning and be greeted by a giant pastry case before getting your latte made to perfection.

of coffee with a thoughtful friend along with a delicious snack, such as biscuits and gravy; sweet potato pie; or, unique to Beacon Hill, a Mexican donut, which is the pastry love child of a traditional donut and a fresh funnel cake.

1600 S Roberto Maestas Festival St.
(206) 453-4892
thestationbh.com

ROXBURY LANES

In the Seattle area, a night at the Roxbury is an entirely different event than what SNL's meaning of the phrase might have you thinking. Replacing bad nineties suits, shoulder pads, and overeager dance steps are two dozen bowling lanes, delicious (although greasy) Chinese food, tater tot nachos (and other American fare), and poker.

It's a one-stop shop for gaming and comfort food in Seattle's South End neighborhood White Center. On any given afternoon, the place might be hopping with children's birthday parties occupying the lanes. Adjacent to the bowling lanes is an arcade complete with air-hockey tables and a pop-a-shot basketball game. On the far side of the building is a legal, nontribal card room offering Texas Hold'em and Spanish 21, and next to that is a low-lit bar and restaurant with hardwood countertops, televisions broadcasting the game, and a menu to put a smile on your face.

Roxbury Lanes is one of a handful of Seattle-area casinos offering, among other options, Chinese fare, but it's also the most fun. While some gaming spots can seem intimidating, Roxbury is something of a family establishment. It's cozy in an odd though pleasant way. There's nothing extravagant about the place. It just offers good, old-fashioned General's Tso's chicken and veggie fried rice.

Roxbury is beloved in the neighborhood by patrons and owners alike. Co-owner Glenda Harrell, who grew up a block away and went to nearby Shorewood Elementary, says she met her husband, Doug, doing what she loves most: bowling. At the time, he owned White Center's Magic Lanes. "He and his former wife and my sister and brother-in-law were on bowling teams for twenty years," she says. "When Doug and his wife separated, my sister asked if I wanted to bowl." They've been married fifteen years now.

The couple bought Roxbury Lanes in 2004 and renovated it, building the kitchen up beyond its original smaller lunch counter.

With comfort food like these delicious wings amidst a gaming paradise, Roxbury Lanes offers bowling, an arcade, and a card room.

Harrell says because the clientele is diverse culturally, she and her husband wanted to serve more than the typical American bowling-alley food. So, in 2006, they brought in the talented Thein Ngo, a former executive chef of the Silver Dollar Casino chain, to create the vast menu. Now Ngo's son, David, manages the bustling kitchen. Hungry patrons can order nachos dripping with cheese, hot pepperoni pizza, or chow mein. The salt-and-pepper wings are beloved. In fact, they won best wings in Seattle on an episode of the Cooking Channel's *Best In Chow*. Indeed, Roxbury boasts a cornucopia of comfort food.

In an area replete with rampant development and business turnover, Roxbury Lanes is a uniquely tried-and-true local favorite. "It's a neighborhood place; that's what we strive to make it," says a confident Harrell, whose son, nephew, and granddaughters have all worked there. "It's not just a job to me," she adds with a laugh. "It's my social life too!"

2823 SW Roxbury St.
(206) 935-7400
roxburylanesbowl.com

TANKARD & TUN

Built in 1996 during the days of grunge music, Pike Brewing Company's classic basement pub, the Pike Pub, located a couple of blocks from the center of the historic Pike Place Market, is adorned with random stickers, exposed grating, and pipes painted black. The pub, which brews and serves some of the city's most recognizable suds, feels comfortable and familiar, like your favorite ripped jeans and flannel shirt outfit, but the famous locale also recently changed significantly . . . for the better.

The folks at Pike recently expanded the space upward, taking over the area above the brewery once occupied by a few retail clothing shops. Occupying the third floor of the building where it's resided seemingly forever, the brewery has expanded its production facilities and opened a new restaurant, Tankard & Tun, which serves succulent seafood, such as fresh oysters and tasty steamed clams, as well as a myriad of the brewery's beers.

"We were at capacity," says Drew Gillespie, the brewery's head of communications, as he shows off the six brand-new sixty-barrel brew tanks recently installed to increase capacity. "This lets us expand a great deal as well as experiment more with new batches. Before, we'd sell every drop of beer we made."

Below, in the pub, Pike offers patrons some 350 seats—an impossible number of folks to serve if they each want, say, a plate of oysters on the half-shell. Tankard & Tun, though, has one-fifth the space, allowing for a more refined experience—but the brightly lit restaurant is not without its kitschy flair. Pike's cofounders, Charles and Rose Ann Finkel, have lined the hallways leading from the center of the restaurant to their brew deck with drinking mugs and steins,

> Pike's kilt lifter beer is one of the oldest and most we'll know craft beers in Seattle.

Left: Each year in the summer, Seattle celebrates PRIDE. And Pike Brewing is no slouch with its delicious Tangerine Pale.

Right: Tankard & Tun, the elegant restaurant in Pike Place Market, was born out of the success of its sister spot, Pike Brewing, two stories below. Photo credit: Morgen Schuler

otherwise known as tankards, for which the spot gets its name—ranging from elegant drinkware to goofy historical-figure spoofs.

What's especially interesting about Tankard & Tun is how much it celebrates craft beer. Beer can often be considered pedestrian, especially in fancy seafood spots, but the folks at Pike want to help promote the idea that beer can be more than that. It can be used as an ingredient, like a spirit, in cocktails, or refined in such a way that the flavors pop and are specific enough to pair with different dishes. During the restaurant's opening celebration, bartenders whipped up a citrusy gin-based drink using Pike's Naughty Nellie Golden Ale, and the menu offers pairing options, such as a purple asparagus salad with cured egg yolk and Pike's Hive Five Honey Ale.

While downstairs the spirit of Seattle's history maintains intact, it's noteworthy that the city's seemingly unquenchable thirst for craft beer has allowed for new upward growth. Indeed, with Pike's development, the old is not being tossed out for the sake of the new. Rather, the new is built upon a beloved foundation.

1415 First Ave.
(206) 812-6619
pikebrewing.com/tankard-tun

BOK A BOK

The road to becoming an accomplished chef is varied. For some, it includes parents in the trade. For others, it's an internship in France, but for Seattle's Brian O'Connor, head chef/partner at the fried chicken spot Bok a Bok, the road began in a trailer park. "I was a fat kid," says the thoughtful chef. "My mom was a lunch lady, and my dad was a janitor and a cook in the army. They weren't really good cooks. There was nothing gourmet happening in my trailer park, but I've always loved food."

O'Connor said his grandfather kept an abundant garden from which he'd pluck ingredients and cook for himself. This tendency eventually led him to working in fine dining for a couple of decades. The chef, who now specializes in fried chicken, grew up in New York (his father was from Manhattan) eating White Castle sliders and bacon, egg, and cheese deli sandwiches.

After finding himself in Seattle, O'Connor worked at several well-respected restaurants, including Quality Athletics, Westward, Skillet, and Roux. "I like to move around," he says, but after offering his expertise to so many eateries, O'Connor's second child was born, and he decided to take a break and be a dad for nearly a year. When he dove back into the fray and opened his own spot, his original hope was noodles, but because of an issue in the lease, O'Connor changed to fried chicken, a move that has worked out to his benefit.

Bok a Bok has since been featured on famed chef Guy Fieri's restaurant show as well as many local media outlets for its extra-

"My mom was a lunch lady, and my dad was a janitor and a cook in the army. They weren't really good cooks. There was nothing gourmet happening in my trailer park, but I've always loved food."

Bok a Bok offers a twist—seasoned to perfection—on traditional fried chicken, and it's worth writing home (or a book chapter) about it. Photo credit: Morgen Schuler

crispy and delightful fare. While many people dub Bok A Bok "Korean fried chicken," O'Connor prefers not to keep anything boxed in. Instead, he says, it's "Bok a Bok fried chicken." No matter how you describe it, the restaurant serves up many local favorites, including a sesame garlic chicken sandwich, kimchi mac 'n' cheese, fresh biscuits, and the classic Bok a Bok crispy chicken wings.

Underlying his love of cooking is O'Connor's passion for teaching and growing his staff, and as he grows his businesses, opening a second and later third location, he wants to continually uplift and inform those who work for him. "I'm really all about mentoring people," he admits. "I believe you can take anyone that has a willingness to learn and bring greatness out of them. My most valuable employees are the ones that began as dishwashers but who are now chefs."

1521 SW Ninety-Eighth St.
(206) 693-2493
bokabokchicken.com

MATT'S IN THE MARKET

When Matt's in the Market owner Dan Bugge bought and took over the beloved, though small, restaurant in October 2005, there was just one window in the place overlooking the historic Pike Place Market. Now, he's happy to report, there are five, and the view of the market and the surrounding water floods in gloriously.

In the thirteen years that Bugge has owned the eatery, the footprint has grown much bigger, including the addition of a full kitchen, and it has increased its number of seats by more than twofold, from twenty-three to fifty-eight. Bugge, who worked for more than a decade in the market as a fishmonger, tossing and catching whole fish, proudly states that his restaurant, which is considered one of the most refined and classic in the Emerald City, is "market influenced," which actually sounds almost like an understatement when considering all the fresh ingredients available on the menu that come from the farmers market below. "We love to support and buy things from the market," he explains. "In truth, we are only as successful as the market around us."

While the source of his menu hasn't changed much over the years, he says, more and more people flock to its natural assortment of vegetables, fruits, meats, and seafood. "I threw fish there for more than ten years," he says, "so I've been in the market for twenty-plus, and every year I'm continually blown away by how many more people come to visit each year. Every time I think it can't get any busier it does."

Certainly one of the reasons for all this tourism is the presence of

> "I love showing off what we have here in the Pacific Northwest," he says. "We have the best ingredients right in our own backyard."

This way to one of the most quintessential eateries in Pike Place. What started as a hole-in-the-wall is now a prestigious restaurant. Photo credit: Morgen Schuler

Matt's in the Market in all its consistent and seasonal glory. Patrons should try the deviled eggs garnished with roe or the pork belly confit banh mi sandwich. Some of the other crisp, fresh fare offered tableside includes plates of king salmon, local asparagus, and fresh, hearty plums. "I love to point out the window and say to a customer, 'Yes, the fish you're eating came from right over there,'" Bugge grins.

Because of his bent toward fresh and local sourcing, which makes up most of Bugge's offerings at any given time, if a family member or loved one visits his restaurant, Bugge says he doesn't bust out a thirty-year-old recipe. Instead, he likes to showcase whatever is recent and seasonally appropriate—perhaps a twist on a new halibut dish, he muses, or oysters on the half-shell from the neighboring Puget Sound. "I love showing off what we have here in the Pacific Northwest," he says. "We have the best ingredients right in our own backyard."

94 Pike St., #32
(206) 467-7909
mattsinthemarket.com

TASTE OF INDIA

Mohammad Bhatti, the thirty-nine-year-old owner and manager of the popular Indian restaurant Taste of India in the Roosevelt neighborhood, says his is a longtime food and restaurant family. The lineage's experience and expertise is evident both in Bhatti's acumen and friendly style as a host and in the homey quality that permeates the quarter-century-old eatery he runs every day.

Bhatti, a more-than-two-decade veteran of the restaurant industry, took over responsibilities at Taste of India when he was just eighteen after his father, who moved to Seattle after stints working in restaurants and hotels in Illinois and Texas, gave him the reins. "I'd been running the restaurant practically on my own anyway," he says. "My father is a pioneer. He's old school. He can't use a smart phone, but he's a multimillionaire."

Over the years, Taste of India has expanded, but it's never really changed, remaining a popular destination for diners and folks just looking for community in their neighborhood. What began as a restaurant using Bhatti's mother's recipes now remains as a landmark to the way businesses looked and felt in the city before massive expansion a few decades later. "We built our customers one by one," Bhatti says. "We specialize in North Indian cuisine, like tikka masala and coconut curry. We innovated a few things, though, like creating our spinach naan."

Other popular dishes, he says, include butter chicken, tandoori chicken, and mango curry. "Our menu is very friendly to gluten-free and vegan people," he says, "but at 85 percent of the tables, it's either butter chicken or tikka masala." It's the consistency and the high-quality ingredients that remain popular with patrons, he says. "We could spend less, like we get our lamb from New Zealand, and it's not cheap, but the quality of the food is really important to us."

Perhaps even more than the menu, though, is Taste of India's quaint living-room feel that keeps its loyal regulars coming back.

Taste of India offers a bounty of traditional Indian dishes, complete with piping hot baskets of delicious naan. Photo credit: Morgen Schuler

"For me, it would be no problem to tear it down and rebuild it," laughs Bhatti, "but I feel if we made it modern, we'd lose customers. They like that rustic, homey feel," which is why the restaurant has welcomed in such famed Emerald City residents as Jeff Bezos, Bill Gates, and even rock stars. "We're low-key," Bhatti remarks. "My dad is good with names but I'm pretty quiet and shy. I just want to treat people well and serve them a good meal."

5517 Roosevelt Way NE
(206) 528-1575
tasteofindiaseattle.com/home/

JACK'S BBQ

Owner Jack Timmons, a former Microsoft higher-up, recently threw himself into the barbecue world. In 2012, he attended a BBQ Summer Camp at the Meat Science program of Texas A&M and later toured the region to pick up homespun tricks of the trade. In 2014, Timmons created Jack's, an authentic Central Texas–style eatery, located a stone's throw from CenturyLink and Safeco Fields in Seattle's SoDo neighborhood, to serve up dry-rubbed meats and delicious savory BBQ options.

Patrons walking through the doors of Jack's will find themselves in front of large family-style tables and an open kitchen showing them just how the magic happens. Once seated, it's best to order a drink. Try the malty, dark-hued Shiner Bock on draft. It's a perfect complement to the spice and char of a BBQ grill. Then it's time for the meal. For starters, order the savory buttermilk hush puppies served with finger-lickingly delicious tartar sauce. Follow that with a chili cup, a thicker, less soupy version of the beloved dish, cooked Texas-style, or, better yet, a Frito pie, which has that same chili atop Frito chips in the bag. Or get the amazing charred rib tips.

Then the real fun begins. The next course from Jack's kitchen should include the mac and cheese, gooey with local Tillamook cheddar and infused with tomato and smoked pepper. Have it next to some of Jack's chorizo-like hot links sausage (spicy and a touch crumbly) and the house's signature beef brisket, a tender, thinly cut, well-seasoned star. Another standout is the cut of ribs, dry rubbed and ready to be ripped from the bone. Finally, as you sit and digest this heavenly meal, ask your server for the Smoked Old Fashioned made with brown sugar, in-house marinated cherries, and smoked oranges, for that final accentuated luxury.

Timmons prides his restaurant on two pillars, he says: authenticity and Southern hospitality. He also believes that

One of the best options at the SoDo BBQ spot Jack's is the hearty, toothsome ribs.
Photo credit: Morgen Schuler

barbecue might just be better in Seattle than in Texas because of "raising the beef in a more moderate climate." No matter where he lived, the Emerald City BBQ entrepreneur would assuredly chow down on the stuff. Barbecue, he says, is one of the food groups that Texans have to eat, and he's right, but it's not only for Texans. It's for all of us.

3924 Airport Way S
(206) 467-4038
jacksbbq.com

CAFÉ NORDO

Café Nordo began, of all places, in the back of a chocolate factory. In 2009, the quirky dinner-theater-that-could started as a pop-up restaurant. The brainchild of Erin Brindley and Terry Podgorski, who met working for the local organization Circus Contraption, curated the experience for two-and-a-half years with a wink and a smirk, using their space to offer theater performances and eccentric meals with the aim of poking fun at the wave of "precious" fine dining sweeping across the city.

At first, in the back of Theo Chocolate in Seattle's Fremont neighborhood (which, incidentally, is a place you should also visit!), the two serviced forty-eight seats. "The concept was 'Modern American Chicken,'" says Brindley. "It was this crazy, avant-garde idea. We had this fake chef coming to Seattle. We made up a whole backstory—Chef Nordo Lefesczki." The couple served a five-course meal highlighting the chicken from egg-to-platter. "We told the press about Chef Nordo, made up a fake resume for him. We even sourced fake quotes from foreign publications."

When Theo needed its space back, the pop-up began moving around, including a stint in Washington Hall in 2012, before landing at its current location in Seattle's Pioneer Square neighborhood in 2015. The current iteration of Café Nordo shows that Brindley is malleable. With high ceilings, big front windows, and hardwood walls all around, the place can fit just about any aesthetic or performance. In the space, Brindley and Podgorski put on two original shows per year, and between those they open the room to

At a recent Café Nordo show, Brindley, the head chef, and Podgorski, who writes and designs the café's original performances, put on a *Twin Peaks*-inspired experience, *Lost Falls*.

Take a trip to a far-off, imaginary land over dinner and drinks with Café Nordo.

other theater companies looking to meld a dining experience into their regular performances.

At a recent Café Nordo show, Brindley, the head chef, and Podgorski, who writes and designs the café's original performances, put on a *Twin Peaks*–inspired experience, *Lost Falls*, which featured a murder mystery with an eerie cast of characters and an expert blend of music, tone, and zippy dialogue. Courses for the show were inspired by breakfast and included an "egg on toast," which was actually a ricotta spread with a "yolk" purée of yellow peppers, yellow tomato, and saffron that was both visually pleasing and tasty.

"It's very, very different every time you walk in here," Brindley says. "It's a completely different world. Transformation feels really important to us. It's our little brick box, our blank slate. We've been able to do some really cool things to make it feel surprising every time you walk in."

109 S. Main St.
(206) 209-2002
cafenordo.com

PAM'S KITCHEN

When Pamela Jacob visited her sister and brother in Seattle for the first time in 1987, she made it a point to carry hot sauce in her purse. "When we went out," says Jacob, "we walked with hot sauces. Everything was so bland in the city!" With a desire for more spice on her palate, Jacob promised herself that if she ever came back to Seattle from her home country of Trinidad and Tobago she would open a restaurant to showcase some oomph. After moving to the city in the mid-nineties, Jacob later made good on her promise after years as a housekeeper, opening Pam's Kitchen on September 22, 2006.

While the restaurant technically serves Caribbean food, more accurately, the 130-seat eatery in Seattle's growing Wallingford neighborhood serves dishes from Trinidad and Tobago with a little Jamaican "twist," says the chef, meaning more added flavor. Jacob, who began cooking as a little girl in her homeland, says she picked up techniques in the kitchen from her mother and other family members. "My passion ever since I was a little girl has been cooking," says Jacob, who ran a little snack and sandwich shop before moving to the United States, "so it's easy when you like something to pick it up."

While there are many delicious options at Pam's, the spicy jerk chicken is at the top of the list. The dish enlivens the tongue, and as the meat falls off the bone, your body is enriched with a sense of comfort food. The curry and roti dishes are warm and inviting, too, and the roti (flat bread), which diners can rip into ribbons and use to pick up the tender, spicy entrees, is second to none in the city.

Pam's has been featured twice on the popular TV show, Guy Fieri's *Diners, Drive-Ins and Dives*.

Left: Enjoy a hearty meal at Pam's colorful restaurant in Wallingford. Food from the mind of a Caribbean chef? Yes, please!

Right: Pam's is a lively, vivacious eatery with plenty of culture woven throughout the walls.

"Everything here has its own unique flavor," says Jacob, who says she thinks of Seattle as home more than any other area she's lived in. "The goat and lamb plates are really picking up in popularity, too, but there are some nights when the whole restaurant is having the jerk chicken."

Pam's Kitchen has called several neighborhoods home throughout its existence in the Emerald City, from the University District to Eastlake to its current location in Wallingford, and while the restaurant has always been appreciated and adored, Jacob says that when she's moved it can feel like a restart instead of a seamless continuation. Nevertheless, she says, the Wallingford business is strong as it solidifies its foundation. "More and more young people are moving into the neighborhood," says Jacob, whose son and daughter both work in the restaurant. "People from California, Idaho. Young people are seeking me out, and they're loving the food."

1715 N. Forty-Fifth St.
(206) 696-7010
pams-kitchen.com

MORSEL

Ever since it opened its doors in 2013, Morsel, located in Seattle's storied University District, has been laying claim to some of the city's best biscuits. The small eatery is half kitchen and half a smattering of seats, but the place feels that it belongs on a New York City corner, with pots hanging from the ceiling and people of all sorts dashing in and out in Uggs and sandals, leaving with paper bags full of the buttery, flakey treasures.

Morsel is a popular location, especially when the neighborhood's Saturday farmers market heats up and people who've bought their organic honey and bouquets of flowers need a bite to eat. For the brains behind the biscuits, what exactly makes a great biscuit? For Morsel's owner, Kekoa Chin-Hidano, the restaurant's biscuit is particularly delicious because of its expertly crafted texture. "I like our biscuits to have a nice crust," he says. "Crumb is too light of a word. I like a little more depth of crispiness than crumb would imply." Indeed, this is very serious science. "And the inside should be almost creamy but not so soft that it's pasty. I want it to be light and fluffy and buttery. Not dense. Dense is bad."

Chin-Hidano, whose favorite menu item at Morsel remains the biscuits and gravy with a fried egg over easy and house-made pickled jalapeños, says the University District has been the perfect place for his business to grow and thrive. Chin-Hidano, who worked prior to Morsel as a computer technician and before that in sales, says the neighborhood is diverse, rich with quirky shops, and welcoming. "And it's great to serve young people," he says.

Chin-Hidano says, "Exposing young people to unique food that people have put some time and effort into is super neat."

Every day Morsel bakes stacks and stacks of biscuits for the hungry University District residents. One look (or whiff) and you'll know why lines go out the door.
Photo credit: Morgen Schuler

"Exposing young people to unique food that people have put some time and effort into is super neat."

Along with the savory biscuits and gravy, standout menu items include the Fast Break, a bacon, egg, and cheese with savory, almost smoky, tomato jam; and the Spanish Fly, an egg sandwich made with prosciutto and manchego cheese. All of the food is warm, eye-opening, and comforting. It's the type of place to visit on a Saturday morning in sweats or the smart to-go spot to visit before a long road trip. "Our vision," says Chin-Hidano, "is just to serve the people well—to serve good food and have it be served by people who care. Things are happening here. It's not dead, not sterile. It's real life."

4754 University Way NE
(206) 268-0154
morselseattle.com

LOTTIE'S LOUNGE

When Beau Hebert and his wife purchased Lottie's in 2010, there was a lot of cleaning up to do. Looking now at the glistening bar or the welcoming tables or the rec room-like corner stage against the eastern wall, you might not believe folks acted nefariously ten years before, but all that is a distant memory now. Lottie's, warmly known as Columbia City's living room, is one of the best places to grab a bite and a beer and talk with a loved one.

"We've slowly made it more and more comfortable for people," says Hebert. "It had been a really uncomfortable situation, especially for the staff, but we also inherited some great regulars, and we've been able to bring some people back who used to love Lottie's. We just want it to be a great place for people to hang out and talk or read a book as opposed to a bar with a million televisions."

The place now is a bustling neighborhood joint with craft cocktails and delicious locally sourced (read: from the surrounding Columbia City neighborhood) ingredients. "Our kitchen is limited," says Hebert, "and we have very little storage space. So that forces us to use really fresh ingredients and local vendors like Columbia City Bakery. When you use high-quality, fresh ingredients, you can get something pretty tasty no matter how you throw them together, and if you do a good job of execution, it can be sublime."

While most of the dishes on the Lottie's menu seem simple, the precision of flavor produced by the modest kitchen is on point and, yes, even sublime—for example, the bacon mac & cheese with panko breadcrumbs, Parmesan, and local Tillamook cheddar cheese. The ingredients are names many have heard of, but the

Lottie's is part of the regular summer showcase known as Beatwalk in Columbia City, hosting some of the city's best instrumentalists in its cozy confines.

The Lottie Dogs may look like muffins stuffed with chocolate chips, but they're cornbread with hot dogs and they're too good to share!

balance is keen, and the Lottie Dogs, like little pigs in a blanket (except the blanket is corn bread), are delicious.

As Lottie's continues to grow, so does the neighborhood around it. Long one of the most diverse areas in Seattle, the South End neighborhood of Columbia City is changing, like many of the neighboring locations in the area. "There used to be a lot more young people around," Hebert remarks. "Now it's more of a young family neighborhood." Yet, he says, the clientele in Lottie's hasn't suffered. "The greatest people come to Lottie's," he smiles, "and we love them for it."

4900 Rainier Ave. S
(206) 725-0519
lottieslounge.com

LA MARZOCCO CAFÉ AT KEXP

Seattle is known for many things, but two of the most prominent are coffee and local music. Everyone knows that Starbucks, the coffee conglomerate, originated in the Emerald City, as did Nirvana, Pearl Jam, and Macklemore, but the city also has many smaller coffee roasters and local bands supplying their skills to city venues. Perhaps the most interesting confluence of these two occurs in the shadow of the Space Needle on the Seattle Center campus in the KEXP 90.3 radio headquarters.

For some ninety years, La Marzocco has made commercial espresso machines in Florence, Italy, selling their equipment to spots all over the world—they'd never owned or operated a café before—but when representatives of KEXP 90.3, one of the hippest indie music radio stations in the world and one of the largest public radio stations in the United States, called, the company answered. They've since established a first-class program in the radio station's pristine public space, partnering monthly with different coffee companies and roasters from Seattle to New Zealand, and with each coffee partner comes a newly designed food menu to pair with the caffeinated experience.

Amy Hattemer, manager of La Marzocco Experiences in Seattle, says the café has partnered with the London Plane, a chic and no-frills bakery in the city. While the café serves mostly traditional fare, such as scones, muffins, and cookies, La Marzocco and the London Plane work to offer specialty food items with each new coffee residency. The menu often features unique toasts, such as a recent salmon cream cheese on toasted rye bread; brown toast with cinnamon, sugar, and butter; toast with strawberry lavender jam; or smashed avocado toast with lemon and lime.

Part of the brand-new KEXP gathering space at the world-famous radio station, La Marzocco provides the coffee and pastries that fuel the day. Photo credit: Morgen Schuler

"We worked with an Australian roaster last summer," Hattemer says, "and so we served a traditional meat pie. We've also served waffles. Our second resident was a partner from LA, and they had these great yeasted waffles."

The piéce de rèsistance for the café, of course, is the proximity to the historic and taste-making radio station. As you sit sipping your drip coffee and munching on your avocado toast, you can see the station's stable of DJs spin records that go out to millions of listeners. If you're lucky, the station might just open up the area to host live concerts featuring such performers as the late Screaming Eagle of Soul himself: Charles Bradley. Not bad for the price of a cookie!

472 1st Ave. N
(206) 388-3500
lamarzoccousa.com/locations/

MOLLY MOON'S ICE CREAM

Molly Moon has a couple of theories as to why Seattle is one of the top consumers of ice cream in the nation, along with such cities as St. Louis, Boston, and Portland.

"Those four cities really celebrate the summer," she says, "because their winters are hard. Also, ice cream is a total winter comfort food, having a pint in front of Netflix. When winters are hard, you buy a lot of ice cream at the grocery store. When you're celebrating summer, you buy a lot of ice cream period."

Of course, all this ice cream consumption is good for Moon. She owns one of the city's most successful chains of ice cream shops, which is also one of the best places for employees to work in the food service industry. Moon opened her first shop in 2008 in Seattle's quaint Wallingford neighborhood, and eleven months later she opened her second location in Capitol Hill. "Opening in Capitol Hill was almost a decision of panic," she smiles, "and it turned out to be a great decision." Ten years later, Moon runs eight shops, with more potentially on the horizon.

Inside, the spaces are spare, brightly lit, and reminiscent of that timeless era when things were simpler and ice cream was everyone's nightcap treat. "As a young woman in her twenties," Moon says, "when I went on a date, I wanted the guy to take me to an ice cream shop after dinner, but in Seattle there really wasn't a good option. That was my motivation!" And so, Moon, working as an executive director for a nonprofit that registered young music fans to vote, wrote an extensive business plan and soon after opened her first location.

The most important question, however, is this: How does she determine which flavors to create and supply to her popular shops? "We brainstorm concepts," Moon says, "things that sound good, taste good. Maybe it's based on something we've eaten at a restaurant or made at home. I have a team of six trained pastry chefs, and we get

This beloved ice cream chain is as classic as it gets. It's the cherry on our Emerald City sundae. Photo credit: Morgen Schuler

together and choose which flavors we're going to do research and development on and put them on our flavor calendar." Yes, if you run an ice cream shop, you have a flavor calendar, and some of the most beloved flavors on that calendar have been honey lavender, salted caramel, strawberry pink peppercorn, and balsamic strawberry.

When you're Molly Moon, you also work to ensure that your employees have excellent benefits—even part-timers—and you have your own employee-based record label, featuring such bands as Seattle's Cataldo, a favorite of Death Cab for Cutie's front man, Ben Gibbard. "I wanted to start a small business with things like great health insurance for all my employees," Moon says. "I spent seven months doing all the research, crunching the numbers. I said to myself, if the numbers at the bottom of the plan are red, I just wouldn't start the business, but the numbers were black, and here we are."

1622.5 N. 45th St.
(206) 547-5105
mollymoon.com

COLUMBIA CITY BAKERY

Quick thought experiment: Where do you buy your bread? Likely, it's at a supermarket or maybe at your local corner store, and yet you maybe carry the romantic idea that if a bakery existed nearby, you'd go out and buy a fresh loaf each morning as if you were a Parisian. Well, if you're lucky enough to live in or near the Columbia City neighborhood, you'd be privy to one of the city's best bakeries, and one whose baguette wins awards year after year.

The Columbia City Bakery supplies three to four hundred loaves of beloved fresh bread to Seattle every day. "Most of the time," says owner Evan Andres, "it just feels like we're baking for some friends, and every night they're throwing a dinner party." The modest steward, who opened his shop in 2005, has a long history in bread baking. For years, he worked in Berkeley, California, studying the craft. That work led him to Seattle, where he continued to study under established bakers such as famed chef Tom Douglas before opening his shop in the city's South End neighborhood. "Inherently, bread is pretty simple to make," he says. "We're trying to coax all the flavors out and take the time that they need to develop. Time is one of the things that gets lost as people are speeding along faster and faster in their lives."

For Andres, there's a mythical quality, even a mysticism, to breadmaking, and it's something, he says, that he can pass down to new generations as he continues to grow his own experience in his little shop. "I want to keep the craft going," he says, "not chasing volume but chasing quality." For the baker, there's a constant, almost platonic, challenge of getting each loaf back to its most ideal form. "Bread is made of the most simple ingredients," he says, "flour, water, salt, and paying attention . . . that's the biggest ingredient."

Andres says his expansive bakery uses a conventional unbleached wheat flour called Morbread that he sources from Grain Craft. "It has

Columbia City Bakery is always brimming with freshly baked goods from sweet treats to classic breads.

great flavor and is fairly consistent," he notes. "We also have a great sea salt from Trapani, Sicily. Our butter is from Crémerie Classique out of Oregon. Our chocolate is from TCHO in Berkeley, California," he adds.

While the Columbia City Bakery, which began to be more and more recognized in town beginning around 2008, doesn't often experiment with its breads—it keeps its standard sourdough loaves and baguettes pristine—it has been experimenting more with pastries, for example, its flaky and buttery croissant and its succulent variety of cakes and Danishes, to much success. "We don't introduce new things breadwise," Andres says. "We're not adding too many jalapeños or cheese or anything. We're just trying to get the flavor of the flour through. That's challenge enough."

In the end, with his efforts baking consistent treats every day, Andres is bringing back the specialty shop in the face of larger and larger grocery stores, much like a butcher or cheesemonger might, to provide a unique, special quality to the bread the city chews daily. "I think that's kind of what I was always hoping for," he says, "not to disrupt anyone's routine but to offer something worth making a special trip."

4865 Rainier Ave. S
(206) 723-6023
columbiacitybakery.com

THE WANDERING GOOSE

Heather Earnhardt, owner and operator of Seattle's Southern-style restaurant the Wandering Goose, said her husband, who is originally from Alaska, had never had a biscuit before they'd met. Well, it's safe to say he's had his fair share by now.

The Wandering Goose, founded five years ago, is a small but vibrant eatery in the popular Capitol Hill neighborhood that serves food inspired by Earnhardt's North Carolina family roots, specifically decadent biscuit sandwiches and giant slices of cake. "I am originally from North Carolina," says Earnhardt, now a longtime Seattle resident, "and I wanted to open a place here in Seattle that wasn't fussy, that people could afford and get big portions of comfort food. I didn't want to serve this precious food you need tweezers for. I wanted to serve food like my Granny used to cook. You can get a biscuit sandwich at a gas station in the South."

Walking into the Wandering Goose, you see tables to each side of the main aisle. It's a shotgun-style layout, long and narrow. To order, you approach the counter and then hope you can get a seat. "We're really crowded on the weekends," Earnhardt remarks. Behind the pastry counter, you'll notice the twelve-inch, three-layer cakes and other delicious pastries, and on the chalkboard above the register are various sandwiches and items, such as the gloriously heaping plate of biscuits and gravy. "There are so many fancy places to eat," says the shop owner. "I think people get tired of that. They want more personality."

Indeed, the Wandering Goose has heart and soul, and much of it stems from the restaurant's founder, who is also the author of a children's book by the same name. The book, which is based on a

"There are so many fancy places to eat. I think people get tired of that. They want more personality." – Heather Earnhardt

As classic as the fried chicken recipes that inspire it, the Wandering Goose's plentiful Southern plates are best with a biscuit and drenched in gravy. Photo credit: Morgen Schuler

true story rooted in a heartaching breakup Earnhardt experienced just before opening her Southern-style eatery, was published by local press Sasquatch books and revolves around a new relationship formed between a little bug and an elegant goose. The storybook, for sale in the shop along with a cookbook from the chef called *Big Food Big Love*, is just another indication of the warmth emanating from Earnhardt.

"I want people to remember the food first and foremost," she says with a smile. "If people come in one time and have the biscuits and gravy, I want them to be thinking about that for a week! So often when you go out, you don't remember anything you ate, but I want my food to be remembered. I believe in food's ability to nourish, to connect people, to cross regional boundaries. I believe a restaurant should feel like home."

403 Fifteenth Ave. E
(206) 323-9938
thewanderinggoose.com

SPINASSE

Stuart Lane, executive chef at Spinasse, one of Seattle's most popular fine dining restaurants, holds dear the history and cuisine of Italy's Piedmont region, where Spinasse gets its inspiration. He incorporates the vegetables and game that would be most prominent in Italy's northwestern region, and one of the restaurant's specialties, its tajarin pasta, has its roots in Piedmont—except that the folks at Spinasse treat their noodles a bit different. "We cut our tajarin dough so thin," explains Lane, who began his second stint with the restaurant in 2013 after a few years' hiatus. "That is very unique. That is not a thing you will see at almost any other place."

Whereas some pastas are a combination of flour, water, and eggs or oil and flour, tajarin is composed of just two ingredients: flour and egg yolks. "It's as simple a thing as you can have," Lane says, and while he believes that he could teach anyone in about a day to make and cut the pasta, it would take "months and months" to be consistent enough to work cutting the stuff in the Spinasse kitchen. In Piedmont, the pasta is wider, Lane says, almost like fettuccini, but Spinasse has changed the dish, turning it into an angelic, melty treasure. "You have to be a hard worker if you want to make the pasta," Lane says, "and you get tiny little improvements and advancements through repetition."

One of the best ways to experience Spinasse is not at the elegant tables around the sixty-seat eatery. Rather, park yourself at the counter in the center of the restaurant, gaze over the shoulders of your server, and watch the yolk-yellow pasta morph from brick-

> "We cut our tajarin dough so thin," explains Lane, who began his second stint with the restaurant in 2013 after a few years' hiatus. "That is very unique. That is not a thing you will see at almost any other place."

Enjoy a plate of mouth-watering, melt-in-your-mouth, delicious tajarin with simple butter and sage.

shaped dough to its eventual bright skinny ribbons. Sip a nice glass of red and enjoy the show, as the dough is stretched and cut with surgical precision. "You don't want to make it look like a machine made it," muses Lane, "but really the highest level of skill are the people who do make it look like a machine made it because they're so good!"

Other standouts at Spinasse are the earthy meat dishes. "Piedmont is a landlocked region," explains Lane, "and back in the day, as the cuisine was being formed, they would make trades with neighboring regions for anchovies, canned tuna, things that can keep—dried cod. In Piedmont, people lived shepherd lifestyles. There was a meat-and-potato ethic. They had some nice crawfish dishes, snails."

In a way, it's funny. While most of the menu is lamb or beef mixed with root vegetables, it is the shining star—the tajarin noodles prepared with simple butter and sage—that continues to make Spinasse's loyal patrons' mouths water. "Now places in Seattle have started emulating us," Lane smiles, "but we did it first."

1531 Fourteenth Ave., Seattle, WA 98122
(206) 251-7673
spinasse.com

MEET THE MOON

Some restaurants are all about the fine dining experience. They're beacons for high-class experiences: twenty-dollar glasses of wine, thirty-dollar entrées. Other spots are unique for their adherence to a certain style or food—Northern Italian cuisine, or Western Chinese—but some places, such as Meet the Moon in Seattle's quiet but beautiful Leschi neighborhood, cater to their immediate surroundings, and to do so, the spot must be both flexible and eclectic in the most welcoming of ways.

"We like a certain environment that appeals to people who live and work in an area, whether that's urban or suburban," says Meet the Moon's co-owner, Larry Kurofsky, of his restaurant company, Heavy Restaurant Group, which owns and operates about a dozen locations in the Greater Seattle area. "When we were looking to open Meet the Moon, we didn't see a lot of options for people in the area, specifically those that could do a lot of things like breakfast, dinner, cocktails year-round."

Meet the Moon is cozy. It's bright and welcoming with charming wooden tables and a long, healthy bar. Kurofsky likes to call the space "intimate" and "approachable." It's the type of place good for a business meeting or a reconnection with a friend you haven't seen in years. "It's nice to see the same people come in," notes Kurofsky. "It can be for breakfast one day, coffee or dinner the next."

The menu at Meet the Moon is sharp and pristine without being too convoluted or pretentious. Whether you're having the baked soft pretzel with melty cheese sauce or a nice, thick burger, there are plenty of options for diners, and one of the restaurant's specialties is its rotating menu of tacos. "We serve tacos every day," smiles Kurofsky. "Leschi is a beach area by a lake, so that was some of the inspiration. Also, I'm originally from Southern California, so fish tacos, tacos al pastor. I love those."

One of Meet the Moon's many specialties is the restaurant's rotating menu of tacos. At this restaurant, it's always Taco Tuesday. Photo credit: Morgen Schuler

The restaurant, which sprouted up in January 2016, has grown and become more and more integral to the neighborhood. It's the kind of spot where you take a seat, and the fellow behind the bar already knows your drink order and can pick up the conversation right where it left off during your last visit. "The more you offer, the more challenging it is to make sure you can deliver and execute at a high level," says Kurofsky, "but having a great and varied menu along with offering excellent hospitality and service are the most important things we can do."

120 Lakeside Ave.
(206) 707-9730
meetthemooncafe.com

NAPKIN FRIENDS

In 2013, chef Jonathan Silverberg was still working his day job, but on his day off, he made the three-hour drive from Seattle to Portland to see about a truck. "This is the day," he remembers saying to himself. "It's real." His friend, who had experience with food trucks, had sent him some listings for a good one. So, Silverberg saw the vehicle, bought it, and took it to the man, just some three blocks away, who would build his new kitchen inside it. "It felt like kismet," Silverberg adds. "Like it was all meant to be." Now, the chef owns and runs one of the most popular food trucks in the Emerald City and one that is also unique. Silverberg, who has been cooking professionally since 1999, had always dreamed of owning his own business, but the prospect of taking out loans and banking on the risk of opening a brick-and-mortar was difficult. He already had the idea—a "good Jewish boy," Silverberg, familiar with the latke potato pancake, thought serving sandwiches with latkes instead of bread would be a smash, and he was right. So, he saved money, bought the truck, and now, some four years later, his work has birthed a successful business. He plans to open a brick-and-mortar Jewish deli in town in the Ballard neighborhood in 2019.

Some of the more beloved items on Silverberg's menu, which he often serves posted outside one of Seattle's popular microbreweries, such as Stoup or Reuben's, include his pastrami sandwich, which he makes from scratch using Nebraska angus prime beef, and the vegetarian sandwich with apple sauce, brie, caramelized onions, sherry vinegar, thyme, and spinach.

The life of a food truck owner, though, is not all latkes and cream. "When you're operating a kitchen on wheels," says Silverberg, whose big blue food truck can be seen a mile away, "it can be difficult. If one of your ovens goes down, you can't still limp by like you were in a traditional restaurant setting. You could lose all your revenue

Sandwiches have a special, toothsome crunch when bookended with thick potato latkes.

for a whole day." But all his hard work is paying off. Silverberg has established his name and his credibility and now can open his next dream spot, the deli.

"If you're looking to grow and have ambitious goals," he says, "food trucks are a good option, but it's your whole life. You have to be willing to sacrifice all your time and all your effort, and without the right people, it doesn't matter what you do. You can't do it all by yourself."

(206) 459-4936
napkinfriends.com

XI'AN NOODLES

In 2014, when chef Lily Wu opened the skeleton shop of XI'AN, known then as QQ Mini Hotpot, in the back of a giant but often empty Korean market, it was clear she was onto something. Wu has been making her very specific, very delicious Western Chinese-style "biang" noodles for years, and finally, after moving a few blocks north on University Way, she's fully established.

To become established, however, first you must learn, and Wu studied for years at the foot of a master noodlemaker and later in small restaurants in China before moving to the United States permanently to set up shop with her husband in 2016. The noodles Wu makes are of a traditional style born in the Western Chinese city of Xi'an, one of the Four Great Ancient Capitals of China. Wu, originally from Songyuan City, a tiny town in northeastern China, left her hometown to pursue an education. She studied to become a teacher but knew if she wanted to come to America—a dream of hers—she'd have to learn a trade she could use in the States. So, she studied the craft of the biang noodle, which, she says, was the first meal she had upon leaving her hometown.

At the time, she didn't even know how to make a dumpling. "I think my mom and dad spoiled me," Wu laughs. "When I went back to China after visiting New York, I knew I wanted to move to America. Young people always think the place near you is not your dream. The far place is your dream." Wu found a teacher who had recently opened a cooking school, and so she studied for six months before working her craft for customers another two years in China.

Now, her restaurant, a sit-down, order-at-the-counter spot with about forty seats, offers the biang noodle with various meat and vegetable toppings, but the star is the simple hot oil noodle, a spicy, toothsome plate that conjures hundreds of years of dough-kneading history in each bite. To make the biang noodle, Wu, who refuses the help of machinery, using only her hands to work the dough, first

Long, hand-pulled noodles are the perfect midday meal you didn't even know you were craving until just now.

works a big ball of the stuff and then breaks it into smaller parts, stretching them out into long noodles. The process, which doesn't even involve a knife, is arduous and painstaking and, in the QQ Mini Hotpot days, only allowed for about three hours of sleep a day for her and her husband.

Despite the long days, however, and a few trips to the emergency room, Wu says she never lost sight of her goals. "You have to be focused," she says. "Focus on detail is the way to make good food. If we're careless, the noodle won't taste good. They're very complicated to make, but the business now is doing very good."

5259 University Way NE
(206) 522-8888
facebook.com/XIANNOODLES/

SKILLET STREET FOOD

Not long ago a study came out reporting the diminishing number of diners in America, specifically, on the East Coast. The findings explained the difficulty of running a diner with a big menu ranging from breakfast to late night, but one business that study may not have taken into account is Seattle's Skillet restaurants, the upscale but very approachable restaurants offering that classic American diner feel but with artisan fare.

The Skillet business, which opened as a single food truck in 2007 but now boasts three brick-and-mortar locations along with a second food truck and future spots opening in the Sea-Tac Airport, offers such food as brioche toast topped with grilled ham, strawberry jam, powdered sugar, and a yolk-dripping egg. It also serves a decadent fried chicken sandwich, giant burgers, poutine, and a lavish brunch menu. The ideas came from Emerald City chef Josh Henderson, who has since moved on from the company to start his own citywide restaurant empire, Huxley and Wallace (named after his two young sons). Skillet, which had been a popular though modest food truck in the pre-cell phone app days, grew massively once Henderson's bacon jam recipe received a write-up from Martha Stewart.

Now, the fifties-style diner, specializing in comfort food, is its own mini-corporation. "When you think about going to eat comfort food," says Skillet spokeswoman Ani Pendergrast, "a diner comes to mind. We have amazing cheeseburgers, fried chicken, and an elaborate breakfast. We make the comfort food fancy, but the diner helps keep us casual. We always walk that line between high-end ingredients with an approachable way to have them."

As Skillet continues to grow, Pendergrast says that the menu continues to absorb new dishes and approaches from other cultures—all as a way of increasing its ability to offer comfort food to its Seattle patrons. "I think that one of the things that's so brilliant

Whether dinner, breakfast, lunch or brunch, Skillet has the fare—like this fried chicken and waffle with pepper honey drizzle—to fill you up and leave you with a satisfied grin on your face.

about our approach to high-end casual food," she says, "is that New American cuisine is branching out in a lot of different ways. Chilaquiles are becoming part of the American menu the same way pasta was adopted by all Americans years ago."

If there is ever a question of what should be on the menu, Pendergrast says Skillet knows where its proverbial bread is buttered. "We really like making food that your grandma would make," she says. "In America, there are so many grandmas that cook amazing food. That's something we're overly aware of as we do our seasonal preparation each year."

1400 E. Union St.
(206) 512-2001
skilletfood.com/restaurant/capitol-hill/

MARINATION

When the great Seattle Food Truck book of the twenty-first century is written, it will assuredly include a lengthy chapter on Marination, the Korean/Hawaiian food-serving vehicle known affectionately as "Big Blue." The business, born in 2009, was part of the early wave of food trucks in the Emerald City and was inspired by the Los Angeles–based-taco-serving mobile kitchen known as Kogi.

"We started a food truck partially because we had a love of street food," says Marination co-owner Roz Edison, who started the business with her partner, Kamala Saxton. "We were inspired by the Kogi food truck in LA, and we knew nothing in Seattle had that flavor profile." So the two did a little research into what the business would take, and in just a few short months, they had their food truck. "We had the idea in February, had the truck by April, and opened in June," she says.

Marination has since blossomed into a handful of storefront locations, including spots in West Seattle (beautifully overlooking water), Capitol Hill, and the burgeoning Amazon campus in South Lake Union. The kitchen offers, among other delights, an array of tacos, from miso ginger chicken to kalbi beef to "sexy tofu," and its infamous kimchi fried rice, served with a sunny-side egg on top.

"We wanted something spicy," says Edison. "We did a lot of testing over and over and over again to see which fried rice dish would work best. All food testing is both a joy and a pain, but you learn a lot about yourself, what you like, and what your friends like." Edison

> "We started a food truck partially because we had a love of street food," says Marination co-owner Roz Edison, who started the business with her partner, Kamala Saxton. "We were inspired by the Kogi food truck in LA, and we knew nothing in Seattle had that flavor profile."

Marination's famous fried rice is worth leaving home, getting in your car and dealing with terrible Seattle traffic and parking for at any time of day.
Photo credit: Morgen Schuler

notes that ingredient and cooking sustainability was paramount with their fried rice dish, which, she says, can fly out the door at a bowl per minute on busy days.

Before securing their food truck in 2009, both Edison and Saxton were in academics. Edison, who had worked in kitchens much of her adult life, was working at the University of Washington as an academic advisor, and Saxton had just finished graduate school in sports management, and it's this background in high-minded and inclusive achievement that drives their business today.

"I think we're really proud of bringing Hawaiian food and culture to Seattle," Edison says. "We're very proud of being an all-woman, all-minority, all-LGBTQ-owned business. When you're a business owner and have 150 employees, which we do, it's your job to educate—to educate young adults how to be professional and comport themselves well; how to teach managers how to keep up a healthy business. We have a responsibility to be examples for our community, and we're trying really hard to do that."

Their food is now enjoyed far and wide throughout the city, from their handful of restaurants to their food truck, often reserved for weddings and birthdays. "Our slogan is Everyday Aloha," Edison says. "That's our culture."

1660 Harbor Ave. SW
(206) 328-8226
marinationmobile.com

OAK

Sometimes you go to a specific restaurant because of the great ambiance. On other occasions, it's those noodles you adore or the amazing parsley pesto they serve with their bread. But sometimes you go to a place not for anything specifically tangible, but because you feel taken care of there. Oak, a neighborhood bar located in Seattle's Beacon Hill, is the kind of place where you get a good burger and a beer and run into a friend, staying a few hours longer than you planned.

Oak's owner, Jeff MacIsaac, a twenty-eight-year veteran of the service industry, was brought in to manage the business but later purchased it. MacIsaac, a lifetime vegan and vegetarian, says his vision for his restaurant is much like his vision for sharing a good meal. "People ask me all the time, 'Your goal must be to own a vegan restaurant, right?'" he explains. "And they're surprised when I tell them no." MacIsaac is not the type to superimpose his own preferences on anyone. He does not want to put limitations on his menu or his restaurant. Rather, he says, he adores running a welcoming neighborhood spot where all are included. "I am just as passionate at making sure our burger is the best that someone can get while also being able to serve a vegan grilled cheese."

Accordingly, Oak's doors are open to everyone, but MacIsaac almost missed his chance to curate the restaurant. He'd chosen to go college—something he'd skipped in his younger years—but when Oak's owners decided they wanted to sell the business, MacIsaac changed his plans and jumped. "Sometimes your reason to leave can be your reason to stay," says the lifelong Seattleite. "Each year I fall more and more in love with Oak. All the time I've spent here, it's become a point of pride."

For MacIsaac, service to the residents of Beacon Hill is Oak's foundational principle. "For the last five years," he says, "I have felt honored to not just be a member of the community and a resident in

Oak is a neighborhood spot in the heart of Beacon Hill where you can just as easily run into a friend as get a great burger and brew.

Beacon Hill but to be able to provide for the neighborhood." While he is passionate about service, he also makes sure the food he offers, from the hefty chicken pot pie to the fried vegan "chicken" nuggets, is top quality. "Every one of our sauces is made in-house," MacIsaac explains, "and all our produce is locally sourced, and all our meats are organic whenever possible."

So, if you find yourself with a hankering for a sandwich and a cold drink, someone to chat with, or just a place to feel human again, head straight for Beacon Hill, enter through Oak's big doors, and let the warmth wash over you.

3019 Beacon Ave. S
(206) 535-7070
facebook.com/OakSeattle/

BETH'S CAFE

The storied though grizzled twenty-four-hour diner on Aurora Avenue near the picturesque Green Lake Park isn't for everyone. "It's a matter of personality," notes owner Chris Dalton, who took over the sixty-three-year old restaurant some fifteen years ago. "The personalities of the people who work and eat here match the restaurant."

The signature dish for the greasy spoon is a twelve-egg omelet served with a myriad of possible toppings, from smoked salmon and cream cheese or veggies to ham and cheese or chili—you name it. But a number of other options are also available, from burgers to waffles and pancakes. Explains Dalton, "We're a breakfast place," and if you need further proof, Dalton will quickly tell you the restaurant goes through "about a ton of hash browns per week" and "about 450,000 eggs a year."

Rumor has it the diner was a former nickel slots parlor, but when the owners saw their patrons get up and leave to eat, they started serving food. Soon afterward the place morphed into one of the Emerald City's most beloved—and oddest—eateries. It's a place where anyone can come in and get a bite. "One of our regulars," begins Dalton, who previously worked in hotel hospitality, "he's usually there most of the graveyard shift overnight. He's schizophrenic, so he talks to himself. So some of the employees decided, because they like him, to wear a blue tooth they found in the lost and found as a way to make the other customers more comfortable."

Any twenty-four-hour diner with tasty food in a thriving artistic city like Seattle will attract the after-hours patrons, who are often half-drunk, and sometimes, Dalton says, on a New Year's Eve you'll

> "Back in the day, it was the grunge scene incarnated," Dalton laughs, "before anybody knew who they were, and now that spirit lives on."

Known for its giant omelets, like this one atop classic hash browns, Beth's Cafe makes sure you're full when you leave.

get a patron not receiving enough attention from her friends and "start doing a dirty dance" by the cash register. This is what comes from a café that came of age during the Golden Era of Seattle rock 'n' roll music. "Back in the day, it was the grunge scene incarnated," Dalton laughs. "Particularly when smoking was allowed, we'd get the grunge crowd overnight smoking cigarettes, drinking coffee before anybody knew who they were, and now that spirit lives on."

As a result of that spirit, tales are woven into the walls of the café. "There isn't anything we haven't seen," Dalton says, noting that tourists visit the well-known spot during the day, but the wild regulars take over at night, "which makes us one of the most accepting places on the planet," he affirms.

7311 Aurora Ave. N
(206) 782-5588
bethscafe.com

DICK'S DRIVE-IN

Dick's Drive-In is a Seattle institution. With its bright orange sign and workers wearing paper hats, the late-night, no-frills eatery is the proverbial flame to which Emerald City patrons flock in droves. The eatery offers a handful of food options, with no substitutions offered, but inasmuch as the restaurant is unwavering in its menu, it's perfect in its simplicity.

And simplicity. is the aim here. Like a localized McDonald's, but one that offers fresh, pleasant ingredients, Dick's Drive-In, founded in 1954, has subsisted virtually unchanged for decades. The result, says Saul Spady, grandson of the drive-in's founder, creates lasting memories for Dick's loyal and hungry customers. "As much as we've changed," says Spady, "one of the most important things is not changing. We want this to be the same burger that your grandmother had, your father had. There's a legacy experience. Memories help connect us in a city literally changing overnight."

If you want an example of how Dick's Drive-In has "changed," look no further than their 2017 menu increase when their famed and beloved Deluxe burger jumped about ten cents, the first increase in years. In other words, the place is practically a time capsule. "My grandfather had three rules," says Spady. "Make a profit, and if you can make a profit, then you take care of your employees, and, third, give back to the community."

Along with their classic American burgers, fries, and milkshakes, Dick's Drive-In is well known in Seattle for what it offers its employees, even part-timers. From maternity leave to college

> Dick's won The Seattle Times Best Burger in 2018 as voted by readers.

The iconic white, blue, and orange of Dick's Drive-In has brought satisfaction to so many people. Photo credit: Morgen Schuler

tuition reimbursement to childcare options, the restaurant chain, which boasts seven Seattle-area spots, is a beacon of responsibility to its staff. "What's important about everything we do is that we're community focused," says Spady.

While Dick Spady, a veteran of World War II and the Korean War, learned how to feed a large group of people on an army base, it was his admiration for quick, consistent food that led him to found Dick's sixty-four years ago, and the template hasn't changed since. "Sometimes it takes a mad genius not to change," says the grandson Spady, "as much as it takes one to invent. The goal of Dick's Drive-In is to be a place where you make special memories. We want to keep having those moments. They're what's most important."

115 Broadway E
(206) 323-1300
ddir.com

THE ALIBI ROOM

Burrowed into the bottom of a 107-year-old building in the former offices of the historic Pike Place Market, the Alibi Room is the closest thing to a speakeasy you'll encounter today. The bar's patrons huddle over cocktails and appetizers in the dark and dim room, whispering wants and wishes as the night winds on.

Corey Ramey and his business partners purchased the nearly thirty-year-old restaurant in 2007. Before that Ramey had worked in fine dining, and before that at Bistro, an Italian restaurant around the corner from the Alibi Room. After shifts at Il Bistro, Ramey would find himself drinking at the Alibi Room bar. "The restaurant had fallen on some tough times," says Ramey. "I remembered it had this cool vibe while also a lot of history. The alleyway right outside the Alibi Room was where horse-drawn carts delivered goods to the market from the water."

Ramey, almost to a fault, has been "fiercely protective" for keeping the speakeasy aesthetic alive and well in his business. "If someone asked me, I couldn't re-create the Alibi Room," he says. "So, ever since we took it over, I've been protective of the aesthetic." Ramey says he pays extra for such things as blank coasters and has paid more to refurbish the handsome wood bar when other cheaper options were available. As a result, the dark, timeless space attracts tourists during the day and cocktail drinkers and industry folks at night.

Fare in the Alibi Room revolves around the wood-fired oven and house-made pizzas, with combos from goat cheese, prosciutto, and arugula to figs and honey, with as many ingredients as

> "I remembered it had this cool vibe while also a lot of history. The alleyway right outside the Alibi Room was where horse-drawn carts delivered goods to the market from the water." – Corey Ramey

Down a cobblestone alleyway in the Pike Place Market, the door to the speakeasy-like Alibi Room can be found across from the historic gum wall. Photo credit: Morgen Schuler

possible sourced from the neighboring Pike Place Market. But the standout item on the menu might be an appetizer: the focaccia and cambozola, served with gooey cheese, a roasted garlic bulb, and basil-topped tomato slices.

The biggest draw—at least for some—is the Alibi Room's resident ghosts. "The Alibi Room supposedly has two different ghosts in it," Ramey says. "Everyone who works here has a ghost story. There used to be tales of the really nice man down by the bathroom who was allegedly the ghost of Frank Goodwin, the founder of the market. Just recently, though, his family came into the Alibi Room and had a little one-hundred-year birthday party for him, and no one has seen the ghost since!"

While ghosts may or may not be your cup of tea, the feeling and historic vibe of the place permeates, whether you find yourself strolling into the Alibi Room right at last call or ordering a pizza at lunch amidst a day of Seattle market shopping.

85 Pike St.
(206) 623-3180
seattlealibi.com

SERAFINA (AND CICCHETTI)

Strolling along Eastlake, one of the prettier thoroughfares in the Emerald City, with its view of the glistening, diamond-like waters of Lake Union and pockets of little shops and restaurants, you will inevitably come on Serafina, a rustic Italian restaurant almost hidden behind leafy green trees and vines in a 108-year-old building.

Inside, you'll see the expansive bar, behind which a smiling face, as if in a timeless photo, will greet you, the bartender's hands polishing a glass or pouring wine. Serafina's menu is rich and plentiful, too, and the eatery has been a jumping off point for many of the city's best chefs, including Unika Noiel and Tarik Abdoulah. Order a drink and settle in before beginning your meal with arancini, or elegant fried balls of risotto overlaid with a light cream sauce. Next, order the caprese with house-made mozzarella and heirloom tomatoes. From the half-dozen pasta options, try the bucatini with pancetta, chili, and pecorino cheese.

Serafina, founded in 1991 by the late Brooklyn-born Susan Kaufman, is the type of place to celebrate something. A first date, a first communion, your first million. It's a chic, swanky place, but it's also welcoming to all, from neighborhood folks to those who just flew in. "Susan was one of those people with immense energy and tenacity," says David Weeks, Serafina's general manager and co-owner. "She sold handmade purses to big box department stores in the fifties in New York!"

The eighty-five-seat Serafina sits adjacent to Cicchetti, founded just a decade ago in 2008. Cicchetti stays open a few hours later than its sister restaurant and focuses, as the name would suggest, on small plates inspired by such places as Venice and North Africa. "Susan wanted these restaurants to feel like your treasured third place," Weeks says. "Come in for a bite of food and a drink or a full meal with the whole family."

Italian cuisine with a particular precision. It's the perfect place for a graduation celebration or a dinner under dim, romantic lights. Photo credit: Morgen Schuler

While you may strike up a conversation with a gray-haired regular or talk about the merits of simple syrup versus sugar in an old-fashioned with the bartender, at Serafina, you will be taken care of before you head back out onto the street toward your next destination. "How many restaurants in Seattle can say they are twenty-seven years old and housed in a building that's ninety-two?" muses Weeks. "Susan always had a soft spot in her heart for the rustic Italian culture she fell in love with in Italy, and it's been her mission from the beginning to bring that here."

2043 Eastlake Ave. E
(206) 323-0807
serafinaseattle.com

BAKERY NOUVEAU

When William Leaman, co-owner of Seattle's Bakery Nouveau, was a boy, he'd often hear a familiar refrain from his mother. "Get out of the kitchen!" Well, says the classically trained baker and operator of one of the Emerald City's most popular confectionaries, "I showed her!"

Leaman opened his bakery, which he co-owns with his wife, Heather, in 2006. At the time, he says, he was "tired of working-for-other time. It was time to do it for us." Before opening his own shop, Leaman had worked at the local Essential Bakery for five years, as well as two years under a master of pastry at the Paris Hotel in Las Vegas, helping to oversee a handful of restaurants, which included baking pies and cakes and, he says, supplying "sugar show pieces" like, say, a castle made of frosting.

"After I left Essential," he says, "I consulted for bakeries around the country. The experience I got from that, helping to generate more revenue for other bakeries, gave me the confidence that I needed to start my own bakery."

Often, says Leaman, bakers focus on one specialty, perhaps, say, a chocolatier or cake chef, but he says he appreciates the wide range to the craft. "Starting in bread," he says, "made me want to know more, learn more. Bread led to breakfast pastries, which led to specialty little cakes and then to wedding cakes. You don't choose the bakery. It chooses you."

Along with the scrumptious macarons, breads, and pastries that patrons line the streets for in his three locations (the first of which was the West Seattle bakery), Bakery Nouveau is known for its twice-baked almond croissant. "People love, love, love that one," remarks Leaman, who says, above all else, that the most important lesson he's learned for success in the kitchen is organization. "It's the key for all success," he adds.

A rich dessert that will transport you to a Parisian café—that's Bakery Nouveau's specialty. Photo credit: Morgen Schuler

As his bakery continues to grow in both production volume and sales, Leaman says he hopes to continue to adapt and evolve. "With our West Seattle and our Capitol Hill locations," he explains, "we serve about ten thousand people a week." The mad scientist continues to innovate, adding chocolate manufacturing and other amenities to his laboratory. "My goal," he says, "is to make the customer feel a part of the process. It's important to see where your food comes from."

4737 California Ave.
(206) 923-0534
bakerynouveau.com

WESTWARD

Chef Josh Henderson, owner and purveyor of several popular restaurants in Seattle, had a specific vision when he designed the scenic, water-inspired gem Westward. "My hope was that it becomes a Seattle restaurant that's around for years and years," he said, "and I think it's got the opportunity to do that."

As of July 2018, however, the future of Westward depends on the bright vision of Seattle chef-owner Renee Erickson and her restaurant group, Sea Creatures, which recently purchased the picturesque spot along with two other eateries from Henderson's own restaurant group, Huxley Wallace Collective. It was a stunning purchase that will allow Erickson to grow her empire and Henderson to spend more time with family. And the announcement may well have culinary ripple effects throughout the Emerald City for years to come.

"When [my business partner] Chad first brought up the idea of us making room under our roof," said Erickson in a press statement, "I told him, 'NO! Are you out of your mind!?' But when I really considered the idea, it made total sense. I couldn't be more excited!"

The chef-mogul has stated that she is in no rush to change anything about the restaurant, which will continue to serve expertly prepared, seafood-focused fare. While some restaurants were founded on trends, Westward, which opened in 2013 and is located in the Fremont neighborhood on the edge of Lake Union, aims for the classic and traditional. The seventy-five-seat restaurant, which can expand another seventy-five seats outdoors in the summer, offers a glistening sunset view for its dining patrons and focuses on a menu inspired by France, Italy, and the Mediterranean—at least for now.

And while the menu is timeless, Westward's layout is a bit creative. Diners often enter their local neighborhood spots and see the building's old-fashioned square or rectangle dimensions. Westward, on the other hand, is all angles and corners inside and expansively

With one of the most glorious views for dining, Westward is a special place, complete with fire pit. Photo credit: Morgen Schuler

pastoral outside. So, whether you're preparing for a jump off the dock into the waters after a private party on-site or hoping to have oysters or a nice cut of fish with roasted potatoes by the fire pit, Westward is a complete dining experience.

2501 N Northlake Way
(206) 552-8215
westwardseattle.com

TAI TUNG

If you ask Harry Chan, grandson of Tai Tung's original owner, Quan Lee, about the keys to success for the nearly eighty-five-year-old restaurant, he will give you a few simple answers. The historic eatery, the menu for which has only grown over the years, has relied on a few tried-and-true methods to sustain its business through many generations.

"We have been here a long time," says Chan, who has worked at Tai Tung for forty-nine years and does a little bit of everything at the restaurant. "We have many old customers, five generations. Our prices are reasonable, and we try to have good service and a friendly environment. That helps."

If you've been in Tai Tung, say, coming in from the rain on a wet, gray Saturday afternoon after some dashed plans, you know there's something more than just crafted hospitality. Sitting in the spot, a pot of hot tea placed in the center of your table, the large, one-hundred-item menu born out of classic Chinese dishes established back in 1935 and grown to meet modern dining demands, the comfort that comes from being a part of well-worn, hard-earned, familial tradition surges through you. It makes you want to eat, to taste the history of the restaurant in each bite.

When your restaurant is in Seattle and more than eighty years old, that means the famed martial artist might even have had a favorite dish. "Oyster sauce beef," says Chan, "that was Bruce Lee's favorite," and at Tai Tung, you can order other favorites, such as pork fried rice, egg rolls, fried won tons, or lo mein, especially palatable for the fan of Americanized Chinese cuisine. Other more specialized favorites include fish in garlic sauce, egg foo young, bean cake, and shrimp balls. Or, if you have a personal favorite, the chefs may make you something off menu. "As long as you tell us what it is, we can try to make it for you," Chan says.

Tai Tung is one of the oldest restaurants in Seattle. Here, you can transport yourself to a different time in the city.

His accommodating mentality is born out of the restaurant that has sustained generations of Chan's extended family. "My grandfather first opened the restaurant here," recalls Chan. "Later on my father worked here, my brother, grandmother, mom. They all come here from mainland China. They all worked at the restaurant. Now my nephew and sister, my children, they all help out," and the hope is for Tai Tung, which has called Seattle's International District home since day one, to continue to support the family, far and wide, for many more decades.

655 S King St.
(206) 622-7372
taitungrestaurant.com/menu

CHACO CANYON ORGANIC CAFÉ

Café owner Chris Maykut says he lives his life honoring three things above all else: people, the planet, and food. It's these tenets that led him to found Seattle's Chaco Canyon in 2003 less than two years after returning to his hometown after a stint working in an upscale vegan restaurant in San Francisco. "That restaurant," he says, "was ten to fifteen years ahead of its time."

Since the age of fourteen, Maykut has worked in restaurants. His career began with washing dishes in Pike Place Market and now has grown to ownership of three cafés. "Food is one of the greatest pleasures on earth," he says, and he puts his fork where his mouth is. One of Maykut's favorite meals—he eats it almost daily, he says—is Chaco Canyon's quinoa, yam, and kale bowl. "Quinoa is high in protein," he says, "and the cooked yams and kale, which are high in nutrients and vitamins, are so good for your body. It comes with this house-made, garlicky tahini sauce with smoked paprika oil!"

When he began in San Francisco, Maykut says he wasn't a vegetarian, but the experience around the food swayed him "for a while." Now, his cafés, which serve all vegan food, the sum of which is 85 to 90 percent organic (the cafés were certified organic for seven years), represent comfortable neighborhood spots where patrons can grab a healthy sandwich or coffee or even a vegan pastry.

Chaco Canyon, though, might not be the place where you want to run in and grab a cup of something. The employees at the register often find themselves wrapped in conversation with patrons wondering about the ingredients or makeup of a given dish, hoping it won't compromise their digestive and dietary needs. "I'm very set on having a place that's a benefit to the community," says Maykut, "and a benefit to the planet. As far as having those conversations about food and diet, that's so integral to me."

Serving some of the freshest, most health-conscious plates in the city, Chaco Canyon has the right stuff to keep your day going.

Being such a niche place, even in a health-conscious city like Seattle, can make for a quirky grind for any owner. "We're a healthy city in a sense," Maykut laughs, "in that we like our hash browns and bacon, and then we go on a long ten-mile hike. That being said, 60 to 80 percent of the people that come into Chaco Canyon aren't vegetarian, vegan, gluten free. They come in here because we have great food."

8404 Greenwood Ave. N
(206) 708-7418
chacocanyoncafe.com

THE PINK DOOR

Jacqueline Roberts began her dream restaurant in 1981 when she was just twenty-nine. "I was really young and very naïve," she says, "but in a good way. Like, 'I can do this!'" So, with a modest amount in the bank—some $46,000 in loans—Roberts began building and shaping what would become her life's work: the Pink Door.

Roberts says she followed one simple, poetic maxim: "I take my walking slow. I learn by going where I have to go." Or, she simplifies, "Basically, it's fake it until you make it." At twenty-four, Roberts knew she wanted to feed people, but she also knew she had other interests, particularly a fascination with cabaret. "Something edgy," she says, "bitey. I like to provoke people." So, Roberts built a little stage and instilled in it—both in spirit and in practice—the risqué.

In the early days, when the Pink Door was just one room— before the bar, outdoor seating, and recent extra-large dining room overlooking the city's luminous Ferris wheel were bought and made to shine—Roberts offered a simple, farm-fresh, four-course meal where diners were served an antipasto, pasta, entrée, and salad dish, but above all else, she says, her secret was in the ambiance. "I pride myself on making a guest feel comfortable," she affirms. "Knowing the synergy between lighting, sound, and temperature of a room is my passion. I pay attention to detail. I'm totally a control freak."

As the restaurant continued to grow within its space close to the Market, Roberts would travel regularly to produce shops and load up her motor scooter for meals. Nights at the Pink Door would go late, with cabaret and other "naughty" entertainment starting as late as midnight in the back part of the restaurant.

While the restaurant now is regularly packed to the brim, when Roberts first began running it, the building's owners "couldn't give the space away," she says, adding that she paid a meager $250 per

Unassuming and hidden in a downtown alleyway, the Pink Door's pink door along an otherwise gray brick wall has become iconic in Seattle. Photo credit: Morgen Schuler

month in rent. In fact, the spot, which features delicate Ahi tuna crudo and decadent squid ink spaghetti with calamari and clams, among myriad other classical Italian dishes, is so popular that Roberts recently instituted a new locals-only reservation policy she calls Club Pink Door.

The thing that sums up the elegant, hardwood-floored, chandeliered Pink Door perfectly is that if you sit outside on the large deck, which overlooks glistening water and the edge of the Pike Place Market, you'll see a giant mural of Emerald City's beloved boylesque dancer, Waxie Moon, painted on a brick wall in perfect view of Roberts's adored eatery, a work of art that underscores her aim of flair and inclusivity. "We want to offer warm-hearted service," she says, "and be provocative."

1919 Post Alley
(206) 443-3241
thepinkdoor.net/welcome

HATTIE'S HAT

In the back of owner Max Genereaux's office is a picture of a keg of beer. It's the very first keg of Rainier beer ever delivered to Seattle after Prohibition, he says. The shot is a perfect cherry on the sundae that is Genereaux's restaurant, Hattie's Hat, an old dive bar with more than 110 years of history in the Emerald City's Ballard neighborhood.

"The place has been going since 1904," says Genereaux, "and lately there are so many new young people to Ballard, but people gravitate toward Hattie's because of what it is, its history. It's not like all these new bars in Seattle that try to look old. This place is real. It is old. It's not made up."

For more than one hundred years, Hattie's—by whatever name it's gone by—has serviced Ballard, traditionally a fisherman's village that for decades felt like home to the loggers, crabbers, mill workers, and other salt-of-the-early surly folk. "Ballard had a Wild West flair after the turn of the century that even the Wild West no longer had," says Genereaux, who owns three historic dive bars (Hattie's, the Sunset Tavern, and Al's) and who first worked at Hattie's in 1996 after leaving a short-lived career in advertising.

Genereaux recalls story upon story of day laborers coming in, slapping down fistfuls of hard-earned cash from long days at work, and buying rounds for the house. "You know how if you ring the bell behind a bar it means you buy a round for the bar?" Genereaux asks. "Well, at Hattie's, there's two bells behind the bar because of the number of people buying drinks!"

"The place has been going since 1904," says Genereaux, "and lately there are so many new young people to Ballard, but people gravitate toward Hattie's because of what it is, its history.

Hattie's Hat harkens back to the fishing village history of Seattle's Ballard neighborhood. With a classic bar, this place has served its share of whiskey.

While the restaurant went through a brief stint as a place for "fine dining," mostly it's been a stick-to-your-ribs kind of comfortable place. Originally, if you walked in around the turn of the twentieth century, you'd be greeted by two barber chairs at the door, a cigar room, a poker room, and the dark, beautiful wood bar. Genereaux has kept to this general feel, tending toward a more dimly lit aesthetic, offering an almost anonymous feel in all the best ways. Nowadays, Hattie's is the place where artists and musicians come before or after a show, plunk down some cash, and get a tall can of beer, a shot of house whiskey, and maybe some pancakes, a baked potato, or fries.

"I could find a chef," Genereaux muses, "say, 'Hey, come be my partner and make this like new Ballard,' and I would make more money, but that's not what I want to do. We're all family here. We love Hattie's because there's a real sense of history that all the staff and all our regulars appreciate."

5231 Ballard Ave. NW
(206) 784-0175
hatties-hat.com

TACOS CHUKIS

Before opening his restaurant, Roberto Salmerón was unsure of his life's next step. Upon graduating college from the University of Washington in Seattle, Salmerón applied for a job at the Gap clothing store to work in retail. The hiring folks there told him they'd call him back after a few days, but he never heard from them. So, he did what everyone would do in that instance: he rode his bicycle from Seattle to Tijuana for an adventure.

"I graduated college in 2010," says the Mexican-born Salmerón. "It was in the middle of the recession, and there wasn't much to do." So, without money for a plane ticket, Salmerón trekked on two wheels to see his family in Mexico. "I missed home, missed the tacos back home. I wanted to see my family and go eat the food more than anything." On his journey, he came to a realization. "Screw it," he thought. "I'll open a restaurant."

At the time, says Salmerón, there wasn't a single authentic taco joint in the city. Taking his cue from Tijuana and Mexico City, the two places with the best tacos in his mind, Salmerón found his modest location off Broadway in Seattle's historic Capitol Hill neighborhood. Since opening that place, he's opened two more: one in the Amazon-centric South Lake Union neighborhood and more recently in the South End neighborhood of Beacon Hill.

The tacos from Tijuana and Mexico City, Salmerón says, are the best in the world because they're done simply, fresh and grilled right in front of you on charcoal. "You can taste that freshly barbecued flavor," says the entrepreneur, adding that at twenty-one, when he opened his taco restaurant, he had "nothing to lose." Keeping ingredients fresh, reducing wasted shelf space, and avoiding having to throw things away is paramount for Salmerón.

While the menu stays the same and has essentially for the complete duration of its existence, each item is perfectly designed and delicious. Favorites include the hearty and lovely pork house

Delicious handmade tacos topped with a little square of grilled pineapple to taste.

tacos; the thick quesadilla with cilantro, salsa, and guacamole; and the toasted tortas. What's the secret to Tacos Chukis' success? "Focusing on one thing at a time," says Salmerón. "I don't like going to restaurants where there's ten pages to the menu. At that point, I'm hungry and I want to be told what to eat. It's so much simpler that way."

219 Broadway E
(206) 328-4447
facebook.com/TacosChukis

BEECHER'S HANDMADE CHEESE

Pop in at any point during business hours at Beecher's Handmade Cheese in Pike Place Market and you'll see the hungry people lining up and sheepishly—or sometimes not so sheepishly—requesting a sample. It's the kind of place you could get a full sampling of all the delicious wares if you were so inclined, and amidst all the gleeful chewing, you'd take a look around and marvel, saying something to yourself like, "This place is amazing!"

Kurt Beecher Dammeier founded Beecher's Handmade Cheese in 2003. At the time, he says, there was no artisanal cheese shop in the Emerald City and if you were to ask residents, they'd say the local cheese was Tillamook. "Which is from southern Oregon and not particularly awesome," says Dammeier. "To me, it said there was an opportunity."

The opportunity, however, didn't manifest to success quickly by any means. "I'd say it took us four years to be an overnight success," Dammeier says. "When we first started selling our cheese at grocery stores around town, it was the most expensive cheese in the store. So, fast-forward to today, even Safeway [grocery stores] has a reasonable selection of cheese. In 2003, that was not the case."

Dammeier, whose shop offers such options as the Flagship (a white cheddar made with Gruyère and Swiss cultures) and toothsome signature curds, says his mission with Beecher's, which gets its milk from Groeneveld Farms in Monroe and Green Acres Farm in Duvall, was to show people that high-quality cheese wasn't just for your "Friday night cheese board," but that it could be an

> "I'd say it took us four years to be an overnight success," Dammeier says.

Beecher's is part treasure trove of locally made cheeses and part sampling haven for your appreciative taste buds. Photo credit: Morgen Schuler

everyday thing, a modest indulgence. "Cheese is a really awesome affordable luxury," Dammeier offers. "Even an expensive piece of cheese, you're not going to eat more than five dollars of it at a time."

While the cheeses themselves are delectable, Beecher's also offers other cooked, savory dishes to its patrons, with one in particular, the mac and cheese, taking on a life of its own. "We call it the 'World's Best Mac and Cheese,'" Dammeier says. "People just absolutely love it," and the positive attention hadn't stopped for Beecher's even after its long-awaited "overnight success." After a few years, the shop was featured by Martha Stewart and Oprah to their respective rabid audiences, and the rest, shall we say, is cheese history.

"I love cheese," Dammeier says simply. "I personally just love cheese both to just eat and to cook with. When we first started, I found the place where we were going to set up Beecher's even before I knew it was legal to make cheese there, and I'm so happy I did."

1600 Pike Pl.
(206) 956-1964
beechershandmadecheese.com

KEDAI MAKAN

Building, sustaining, and operating a restaurant often necessitates true love and passion. The effort to grow the endeavor and balance all the responsibilities cannot be sustained unless the proprietors are invested mind, body, and spirit, and this is certainly the case with the Malaysian restaurant Kedai Makan and its hardworking cofounders, Kevin Burzell and Alysson Wilson.

What began in a booth in a Seattle farmers market grew after a year into a brick-and-mortar take-out window in the Capitol Hill neighborhood and soon after, into a traditional sit-down eatery, as it is now. At the farmers market, Burzell and Wilson would offer a rotating three-option menu. "On our first day," remembers Burzell, "we did hakka noodles with ground pork, sprouts, and a chili sauce; a nasi lemak with coconut milk; and a lor bak, which is seasoned pork in bean curd skin, deep fried."

While Kedai Makan's operators love food, it's the simple but profound diversity of the country where the food originates that especially enlivens their creative efforts. "We try to bring the diversity of Malaysia to the menu, to the decor, the music, everything," Burzell says. "What we love about the country is the diversity of people. It's all right on the streets."

The two, who have been romantic partners for more than a decade, traveled to Southeast Asia a number of times and felt compelled and challenged by its cuisine. "We thought," says Burzell, who's worked in restaurants since he was fourteen, "it's time to give it a try cooking it." So, without any money, they began at the farmers market. "We worked hard and enough people enjoyed it," he says. "We slowly saved and slowly built."

One of the standout menu items at Kedai Makan is the nasi goreng kedai, which is darkened, dense (in the best possible way) fried rice cooked with tofu, sprouts, greens, and a fried runny-yolk egg on top.

In the small, quaint Malaysian Kedai Makan, rich flavors and dishes abound in this visually appealing Capitol Hill hot spot. Photo credit: Morgen Schuler

"You won't really see that served in a restaurant or at a street stall in Malaysia," Burzell says. "It's more of what a mom would make for a normal meal." Burzell says the restaurant uses a dark, thick, sweet soy sauce called kecap manis, almost like molasses, and the trick he says is frying the rice slowly so that it can build caramelization. The dish is one of the many reasons to visit the well-cared-for spot. "We got really lucky getting both spaces on Capitol Hill," Burzell says. "Things fell into the right place at the right time."

1802 Bellevue Ave.
kedaimakansea.com

GAINSBOURG

When co-owner JJ Wandler opened his dark noir bistro in Seattle's Greenwood neighborhood, he wanted to create a traditional French restaurant, but not the highfalutin kind that is more fancy than authentic. Rather, Wandler wanted to open the kind of place regular French neighborhood folks would go.

"I wanted the atmospheric things I'd seen in French New Wave cinema," Wandler says, "and the biggest praise I've gotten from French people is that it feels like their favorite bar in France. Not an amusement park version of a French place."

Things were not all hunky-dory, though, for the restaurateur. When he opened Gainsbourg, named after the famed French musician and director, in 2008, the surrounding neighborhood wasn't as built up and quaint as it is now. "When we moved into our location," Wandler says, "the philosophy was, 'Let's try to be the nicest place on the worst block.' There were a lot of empty storefronts, which is not true any longer."

Now the area matches the flair and candlelit allure of the French eatery, and if you wanted further proof besides the continuous loop of the black-and-white French films projected on the far wall, try the escargot, which Wandler hopes many actually will. "I'm a big fan of escargot," he says. "When we opened, snails were typically going for twelve dollars [a plate], but we've been selling six for four dollars at our restaurant so that people who've never tried it before wouldn't feel priced out. We've ended up turning lots of people onto the dish."

Other top dishes include the beef and lamb burger made with caramelized onions and the dark, rich French onion soup, the recipe for which Wandler says he and his staff have been perfecting since the spot's first day. "When we opened nine years ago," he says, "our

"I wanted the atmospheric things I'd seen in French New Wave cinema," Wandler says.

A decadent, giant burger with a fried egg on top is just one of the many finger-licking delicacies at this artist-inspired, dimly lit gem.

French onion soup needed a lot of work, but we'd had multiple folks in the kitchen over the course of those years, and I've always said, 'If you have an idea that would make this better, then let's give it a shot.'" As a result, the soup includes traditional beef stock, sherry, thyme, and a delicious Gruyère crouton.

And so Gainsbourg thrives, albeit after a rough start. While Wandler signed the lease during the 2008 economic downturn and faced many questions about the viability of his dream spot, the restaurant exists and is a shining light in its increasingly developing neighborhood. "I knew I wanted to own a French dive bar," he recalls. "It really had to do with the space feeling like it would lend itself to the name and the theme I envisioned, and then, thankfully, I found it."

8550 Greenwood Ave. N
(206) 783-4004
gainsbourglounge.com

EASY STREET CAFE

Concerning Seattle's popular music scene—whether for you that means the eighties, nineties, or the opening years of the new century—the West Seattle café owner Matt Vaughan has seen it all. The man who opened Easy Street in 1988 after working in two other record shops and dropping out of Seattle University opened the café inside in 1999 as a means to grow his dream during a difficult time in the music business.

"At the time, in the late nineties," says Vaughan, "there was a lot of talk about the death of the record store. There was the issue of big box stores to contend with, the rise of Amazon, peer-to-peer file sharing like Napster. I was getting a little leery myself. I had to be concerned with the future of Easy Street. We had to create something that would be unique, authentic, and make us impervious to our competition and the industry challenges."

So, Vaughn purchased the space, which was formerly Joe's Grill, next door to his record shop in 1997. "At the time," he says, "I was either going to invest in more record store space or utilize the hood system that was already there and upgrade the kitchen and create a café," he explains. "I struggled with that notion, though, because I wasn't a chef and had never worked at a restaurant, but my friend Pat Tunison helped me create the initial recipes. The menu was inspired by a ski trip I did from Taos to Seattle after missing my flight from Albuquerque: breakfast burritos, hashbrown scrambles, egg sandwiches, corned beef hash."

Success for the eatery didn't come quickly, however. While records, CDs, posters, and other musical memorabilia surround the café, Vaughan says it took a while for people to get used to the idea. "It was

Easy Street has hosted live performances in the shop for years. From bands like The Sonics to Macklemore & Ryan Lewis to Shabazz Palaces.

Easy Street is the quintessential Seattle record store. It's packed with vinyl albums and made complete by a great café smack-dab in the middle.

a struggle for the first couple years," he says. "It took people a while to realize what an eatery was doing in a record store." But now the shop, which features themed menu items such as the plentiful Woody Guthrie Farmers Omelet, hearty New Wave O's Rancheros, healthy Hall and Oates, and scrumptious Soundgarden Burger, does quite well, and it has even helped foster the careers of some of the world's most well-known players.

When the café first opened, Vaughan says, early supporters were such musicians as Chris Cornell, Eddie Vedder, Andy Parypa of The Sonics, Chris Ballew, Fleet Foxes, and a young busker named Brandi Carlile. "It has always been a place where the music is what attracted the early customers," he says. "It just so happened that the food and coffee was damn good. In a world of social networks and the digital revolution, people yearn for real-life contact and neighborhood legitimacy, and we get a great crossbreed of ages and types of people coming in. People who like food, most of them like music, and those who love music have to eat!"

4559 California Ave. SW
(206) 938-3279
easystreetonline.com

THE WEDGWOOD BROILER

Walking into the restaurant, you'll think, "Wait, did I just go through a time warp?" While you didn't actually go through one, you kind of actually did. The Wedgwood Broiler, founded in 1965 in the sleepy Wedgwood neighborhood, looks almost exactly the same, from menu to bar top to carpet, as it did on day one some decades ago.

Derek A. Cockbain, who grew up in Wedgwood and went to high school at Seattle's Nathan Hale, purchased the Broiler in 1996 after working in the kitchen upon graduation in 1980. "I wanted to preserve the place," he says, reflecting. "It was a long-standing business, and I thought owning it could be a really good thing. Now I'm living the dream."

The interior of the restaurant is as classic as a baked potato with butter, chives, and sour cream wrapped in aluminum foil, which, it's no coincidence, you can order off the menu to your heart's content. Other items include classic cheeseburgers, onion rings, quesadillas, and the house salad, which is topped with bright orange, satisfying Cheez-Its. "People always make mention of that," laughs Cockbain. "For better or for worse."

While most of the Broiler's customers are regulars from the neighborhood, the place sees its fair share of new patrons, especially after a local publication writes the place up with the gentle flair of nostalgia, and Cockbain says he wants those customers—both new and old—to "leave happy and full" while also enjoying the vintage aesthetic of the Broiler. "We've had a good thing going for fifty-three years," he says. "Why change it?"

He's stuck to this rhetorical question through the two decades he's run the spot. Inside, you'll see couples married for fifty years or a local rock band celebrating post-gig or two youngsters on a first date canoodling in a booth over a shrimp cocktail. "It's fun to see the new

Many of the classic entrées at the Broiler offer a side house salad, notable because each salad comes with Cheez-Its—and nothing could be better!

customers that come in, look around, and say, 'Jeez this place looks like it's from the sixties!' Well, it is. We've kept that deliberately. You don't find many bars that look like ours."

So, pull up a bar stool, order a mixed drink from one of the women who've worked the spot for years, get a salad with some Cheez-Its, and relax. Because the more things change, the more they stay the same, especially at the Broiler.

8230 Thirty-Fifth Ave. NE
(206) 523-1115
wedgwoodbroiler.com/index.html

NAKED CITY BREWING

The story behind Naked City Brewing, from its array of freshly brewed beers to its revamped and delicious food menu, begins with, well, stories. "We got our inspiration from an old movie," says co-owner Bryan Miller, who joined the brewery in 2011 shortly after it opened in 2008. "It was called *The Naked City*, a 1948 film noir. It was the first studio film shot on location. It blurred the lines between life and art."

The slogan for Naked City Brewing is "Every beer tells a story." Indeed, on the beer menu, each beer listed comes with a blurb about its origin, and this is apt given Miller's history. He's a graduate of New York University with a master's degree in poetry, and the brewery carries on its storytelling theme beyond the pints it brews into its dining area, which comes complete with a stage set for performances, such as live podcast tapings, radio shows, and acoustic performances akin to VH1 *Storytellers*.

Along with the artsy side of things at Naked City, the founders aimed to carry on the tradition of the American public house. "When the colonies began to grow in New England," Miller recounts, "there were two public buildings: the church and the public house, or local pub." So the place is a gathering spot for many in its surrounding Greenwood neighborhood and beyond.

Menu-wise, Naked City has grown leaps and bounds since its early days. What started as simple cold meat and cheese plates spread out to soup and sandwiches, but Miller says the brewery's patrons demanded even more than that. "People were hungry, and the place was full," recalls Miller. "So we put in a full kitchen and hired our first executive chef in 2012." That chef, Tessa Roberts, revamped the menu. Most of the items, except for a couple of staples, such as the bread, are made from scratch in-house, Miller says. "We shoot for gourmet comfort food," he adds.

Come for the freshly brewed pints of beer and stay for the savory fare that includes giant baskets of fries and darn tasty burgers. Photo credit: Morgen Schuler

Naked City cuts about three tons of potatoes per year for its ample baskets of French fries, Miller says. "The potato delivery guy doesn't like us very much," he laughs. Other items include the warm pretzel made from spent grain and served with stone-ground honey mustard, the classic Naked Burger with grass-fed beef (suggested pairing: IPA), and the vegan beet burger with spinach (best with a pale ale). The kitchen even uses the beer as an ingredient in such dishes as the house salad made with candied walnuts and house-made beer vinaigrette.

The main reason to go to Naked City, though, is to drink a glass of your favorite something with your meal and feel a part of the neighborhood, much like Greenwood local Terry does. "Terry has her seat at the bar," Miller explains, "with her name on a plaque. She loves old movies, and instead of sports, we play old movies on the TV in the bar. She loves who we are, what we're about. We call her house if she doesn't come in for a day. Then when she's done, she takes the bus one stop away. She's family."

8564 Greenwood Ave. N
(206) 838-6299
drink.nakedcity.beer

THE CARLILE ROOM

In the three decades since he's owned and operated his restaurants in Seattle, Chef Tom Douglas has learned a few important lessons regarding both customer service and service to the environment. Douglas, who owns more restaurants in the Emerald City than can be counted on two hands, opened one of his latest, the Carlile Room, in 2015, and the dimly lit, vegetable-forward bar and eatery, named after the prominent local folk songwriter Brandi Carlile, is an example of how Douglas is both a successful businessman and a steward of local food culture.

Located next to the city's famed Paramount Theatre, the Carlile Room, initially inspired by singer Bob Dylan and the generation in which he rose to fame, serves the theater crowd as well as a growing population in the downtown area. "In my mind," says Douglas, who acquired a Bob Dylan set piece from the Grammys one year that he used as the model for the restaurant's aesthetics, "the Carlile Room was inspired by flower power, the late sixties, and all of the things going on in our country—both good and bad—at that time. You had racial tensions, Martin Luther King Jr., the Kennedys, Vietnam War issues, hippies, all those sorts of things."

The Carlile Room, which is open seven days a week beginning at 4:00 p.m. and offers popular dishes, such as retro homemade onion dip with chips, hushpuppies (Carlile's favorite) with duck liver mousse, and rotisserie-cooked dishes with chicken, duck, and pork, is the type of place you hunker down after a show with a cocktail and a plate of rainbow vegetables and discuss what you just saw. It's a place to chew over the work while chewing on a snack, and it's born out of the decades of experience Douglas has earned in the Emerald City. "For me," he says, "undertaking a new restaurant means undertaking the whole process—from financing to figuring out what a neighborhood needs to marrying what I had in my pea brain with the actual design."

Oh, no big deal, just a giant selection of delicious brunch options at the Carlile Room.

    With those well-earned decades of experience, Douglas, who says he got the okay to name the cozy spot after Carlile over a shared dinner, says he is also in the unique position to "preach" a little to his fellow chefs and highlight what's important for local restaurants, including the Carlile Room, as well as the local environment his restaurants benefit from. "After the amount of time," he says, "that I've been in the restaurant industry, I think it makes me qualified in a funny way to preach a little about taking some action when it comes to our environment. I'm in the position where I can help round up my fellow chefs, and we can try to focus on what's important in our food chain and how we can be more helpful to it."

820 Pine St.
(206) 946-9720
thecarlile.com

TANKARD & TUN (page 10)

CAN CAN CULINARY CABARET (page 2)

JACK'S BBQ (page 18)

GAFÉ NORDO (page 20)

Libido

MULTIGRAIN
SUNFLOWER
$6.00

WALNUT
FICELLE
$3.25

SOURDOUGH
BOULE
$5.50

ROASTED
POTATO
$5.90

CIABATTA
SANDWICH
ROLL
$1.50

PLAIN DINNER
ROLL
$0.75

COLUMBIA CITY BAKERY (page 32)

NAKED CITY BREWING (page 82)

LA ISLA (page 154)

OOINK (page 162)

HOTEL ALBATROSS (page 178)

JUNEBABY (page 116)

THE GARLILE ROOM (page 84)

THE WHALE WINS (page 182)

WALLYBURGER (page 176)

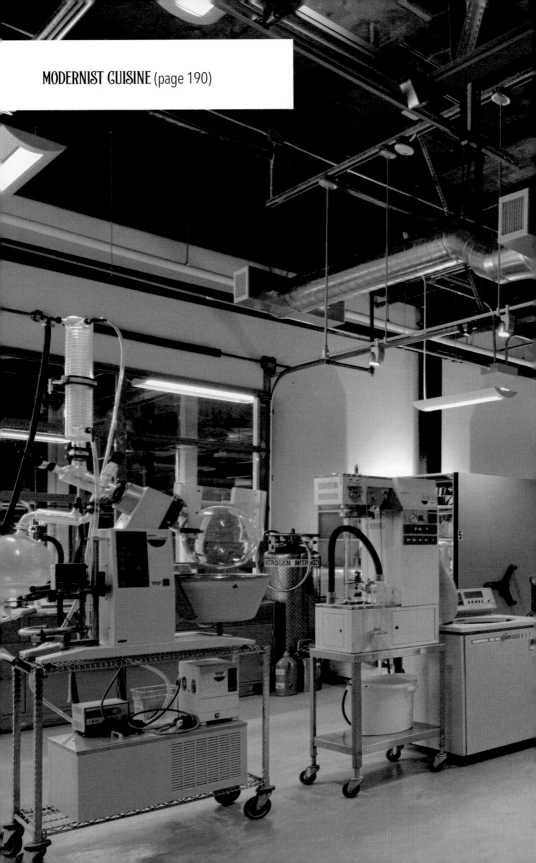

CAPITOL CIDER (page 150)

EASY STREET RECORDS CAFE (page 78)

NUE

Owner Chris Cvetkovich, who cofounded Nue with his wife, Uyen Nguyen, is a traveler. He's visited more than eighty countries, and in those visits, especially during some long excursions with Uyen, he realized something: creating a place where people of all sorts can come together to enjoy the best street food dishes from around the world is his passion.

"We get our recipes from everywhere," Cvetkovich says. "From different countries and from our line cooks and dishwashers. If it's a cool idea, we want to try it."

Cvetkovich says he would find himself abroad and seeing signature dishes in various locations that were staples to entire countries, but after returning home to America, those dishes could never be found. "Most people think that if you go to Bulgaria and have a great dish and you want to come to America to cook and sell it, you have to open a Bulgarian restaurant," he says, "but you don't have to do that. I wanted to be able to handpick my favorite dishes and offer them in one place."

Nue features food from all corners of the world, from the Caribbean to Africa to Asia. A former 3D artist for video games for the likes of Xbox and Playstation, Cvetkovich, after traveling to twenty-three countries in five months with his wife, said he just couldn't do that work anymore. So, with a love of food and cooking in his back pocket (after work, he'd come home and often cook), he took the plunge and opened the restaurant. "The day we got back," he says, "we started looking for locations."

"We get our recipes from everywhere," Cvetkovich says. "From different countries and from our line cooks and dishwashers. If it's a cool idea, we want to try it."

Nue, as the phonic sound of its name might suggest, always has something new to offer its patrons. Its menu is as adventurous as the eatery's customers.
Photo credit: Morgen Schuler

Nue's menu rotates items, but Cvetkovich tries to keep the beloved, tried-and-true options consistent—dishes such as the South African bunny chow (chicken breast, masala, lime, and cilantro served in a bread bowl), Balinese barbecue ribs, and the Chengdu spicy jumbo chicken wings. Other items include balut (a partially developed duck egg) and Burmese laphet toke, which is a fermented tea leaf salad. "We try to stay original," he says. "We don't 'Americanize' anything."

Perhaps more than the menu, what symbolizes Nue the most is its large, wooden communal tables. "People love the communal tables," Cvetkovich says. "What I love about Nue is we had this concept. We were sitting in this place in Portugal, a small dive bar that served food to people of all kinds. That's what we wanted to open: a communal restaurant and pub that had old people, young people, people of different nationalities, all getting together. You can't make that happen, but we feel lucky it did."

1519 14th Ave.
(206) 257-0312
nueseattle.com

PATTY PAN GRILL COOPERATIVE

Patty Pan founder Devra Gartenstein went through a number of other business iterations before landing on the delicious, rustic, and satisfying experience that is her farmers market grill. She started as a food entrepreneur in 1997, but it was in 2003 that her ambitions were realized.

"We're now at thirteen farmers markets," Gartenstein says, but why is her fare so popular? "We do something that we believe in. We're sincere about it, and we bring that to every part of the business, from being a worker co-op to having really strong relationships with the farmers who provide our ingredients."

While many of Seattle's best eateries range from the fancy to the fantastical, Patty Pan keeps both feet planted firmly on the ground. The organization's best-selling item is its quesadilla, comprising a giant tortilla, a mixture of freshly cut and cooked vegetables, and two generous handfuls of shredded cheddar cheese. "We first started with just tamales," Gartenstein says. "At a certain point, we added vegetables to the tamales. Later, I had some leftover tortillas and some leftover cheese, so I took it to the market one day, and really it's the best thing we've ever done." Top the quesadilla with the homemade ancho sauce and you'll taste simple divinity.

As a worker-owned cooperative, Patty Pan, says Gartenstein, is a workplace democracy with shared revenue and shared responsibilities. While their locations are the very mobile tents and grills, they have a home base in Shoreline, with a commercial kitchen

"We do something that we believe in. We're sincere about it, and we bring that to every part of the business."

A Patty Pan grill is like no other. Steam rising from an amalgam of fresh veggies never looked so good!

and a small dining room in which they host local food community dinners once a month. Their food is available year-round at the Ballard, University District, and Capitol Hill weekly markets.

"I think our following is unpretentious," Gartenstein says. "I think our food is wonderful, but it's really straightforward. We don't show off. We just want to make a great product and put it out there at a fair price. We support farmers because many of our ingredients come from farmers. By supporting us, our customers are supporting farmers, and I think that's part of the appeal."

Look for the long lines at the local market to find Patty Pan. You'll see someone with a big metal spatula in hand flipping grilled tortilla after grilled tortilla filled with beets, greens, carrots, and a myriad of other healthy, farm-fresh vegetables bonded with melted cheese. Carry the food around as you shop for wine, cheese, or your own fresh veggies, and remember that while there are many options for the fancy, to do something simply and honestly, that's a natural meal. "We love what we do," says Gartenstein.

15550 Twenty-Seventh Ave. NE
206-782-1558
pattypangrill.com

LUNCHBOX LABORATORY

If you ask Lunchbox Lab's executive chef, Evan Poulias, just about anything can be made into a burger or a milkshake, and if you go to Lunchbox Lab in Seattle's South Lake Union neighborhood, you'll see that he's absolutely right.

Some of the specialty items on the menu of the restaurant, which prides itself on its fun and playful twists on American classics, include the Dork Burger (with a patty made from duck and pork) and the Cinnamon Toast Crunk milkshake (made with Cinnamon Toast Crunch cereal and Fireball Cinnamon Whisky). "Our philosophy is to take a fun approach," says Poulias. "'Experiment' is one of the words we like to use. We like to go outside the proverbial box."

The idea behind the establishment is to excite the imagination as if each diner is a little child that, at least in some ways, is allowed to play with his food. Those French fries become rocket ships, the milkshakes the Milky Way. "The point is to let your mind go," Poulias says.

While the essence of Lunchbox Laboratory is playful, the roots of the restaurant rest in some sadness. Original founder Scott Simpson established the eatery at a hole-in-the-wall in Seattle's Ballard neighborhood and often had a line out the door. In 2011, Simpson ended his life, but his original idea, to literally play with his food, lives on. "He was a super-creative guy," recalls the executive chef, "and we're now an expanded version of what he originally conceived of, with more offerings. It's even wilder."

One of the menu items at least zigs where the restaurant zags: its homage to the classic Dick's Deluxe with added bacon and Top Secret Burger Sauce. "All of us think they do a fantastic job," Poulias says, "and we just wanted to take a fun spin on their standard." Yet, while those at Lunchbox Lab appreciate their Emerald City history, Poulias says he also appreciates when people

In one way, you'll never know what the next burger on the menu will be topped with. But you'll always know it's fantastic. Here, you're encouraged to play with your food!
Photo credit: Morgen Schuler

outside of Washington show their love. "For me as a chef," he says, "there's no greater satisfaction than somebody enjoying your product. It's very humbling."

1253 Thomas St.
(206) 621-1090
lunchboxlaboratory.com

FRANK'S OYSTER HOUSE & CHAMPAGNE PARLOR

When restaurant co-owner Sarah Penn was a little girl, her grandfather, Frank, would get dressed up and take her out to a nice restaurant. Now, Penn is keeping that feeling alive with her neighborhood spot, Frank's Oyster House & Champagne Parlor.

The establishment, located in the Ravenna-Bryant neighborhood, is cute and quaint. In some ways, it feels part New Orleans and part Alice in Wonderland, with throw pillows in the windows and po'boys on the menu. "It's interesting," says Penn, who opened up Frank's with her husband, Felix, in 2009. "Our inspiration comes from a blend of things." The two also own Pair, a chic restaurant in its own right, located three blocks east of Frank's. "It's a modern rendering of an East Coast oyster house. New Orleans does come into play too. My dad was from the South, and that's a source of original American cuisine."

While Penn is from Seattle, she spent significant portions of her life in San Francisco and on the East Coast. As a result, she picked up sensibilities from these locations, and all are a part of Frank's, but the main inspiration behind the place, she says, was the dearth of local, independent oyster restaurants in an area famous for oysters. "In 2009," she says, "everyone was obsessing with the economy and rightfully so, but we were trying to tell people oysters and champagne were right for a neighborhood restaurant."

While the takeoff was tough, Penn says after about six months they hit their stride. "We bonded with the neighborhood," she says.

> "In 2009 everyone was obsessing with the economy and rightfully so, but we were trying to tell people oysters and champagne were right for a neighborhood restaurant." – Sarah Penn

Frank's is a lovely little gem hidden in the sleepy Ravenna neighborhood—part neighborhood watering hole, part Alice in Wonderland tearoom.

"Our cocktail lounge really was especially good timing. People were ready to have craft cocktails in their backyard," but it was that proverbial backyard that proved both inspiring and challenging to the couple as they were building Pair and then Frank's. The Ravenna-Bryant neighborhood is simple but complicated. It's sparse, devoid of the commercial density that, say, the Ballard, Fremont, and Capitol Hill neighborhoods have, but it's close to wealthier neighborhoods and is rife with families and young professionals. "When we first started, there was nothing here," Penn says. "So we did it."

Despite Frank's small size, the menu is bountiful. It features a rich, decadent brunch featuring made-to-order donuts with berry coulis and mascarpone cream, dinner with local salmon or New York strip loin, and an elegant happy hour with poutine and po'boy sliders. "When we'd go out to eat," Penn recalls, "my father would always have a manhattan. It was a special occasion but not necessarily *for* a special occasion. Frank's is a tribute to that."

2616 NE Fifty-Fifth St.
(206) 525-0220
franksoysterhouse.com

REVEL

When Seattle diners first caught wind that Revel would be closing, shock ensued, but there's good news to come with the announcement. In the year during which the Korean fusion restaurant's landlords will be remodeling the Fremont building in which Revel resides, the restaurant will be running a pop-up version—Revel 1.5—in the Emerald City's downtown neighborhood. There, chef/owner Rachel Yang will experiment with a few new options as she prepares to move Revel back to her original home base, where she opened the famed spot in 2010.

While the items on the menu frequently rotate, Yang keeps the same five categories, adhering to the idea that good food is most approachable through simplicity and familiarity, and street food is the inspiration for the establishment. "Korean comfort food," Yang underscores. "The menu is very small: salads, pancakes, dumplings, noodles, and rice bowls. Street food connects with everyone, and everyone feels very casual trying it."

Revel has some of the city's best food. Two items no diner should miss are the angelic Dungeness crab seaweed noodle (served with red curry and crème fraiche) and the succulent short rib dumplings. "Short rib is Korea's favorite cut of meat," Yang says. "It has the perfect balance." Revel uses soy sauce, sake, chili, ginger, and garlic to infuse and bring out the flavors in the meat before wrapping everything in a toothsome dumpling casing. Another standout item is the albacore tuna rice bowl, served with fennel kimchi, escarole, and an egg yolk for you to break and mix into the bowl's contents. "People are saying they're going to miss the food while we're gone," laughs Yang.

Surely, the menu will be missed but so, too, will the restaurant's charming physical space. With outdoor deck seating (complete with heat lamps for Seattle's chilly evenings) complementing the long, indoor counter at which diners can sit, one can only hope the

Korean options abound at the gloriously rich Revel, including handmade dumplings and green onion pancakes.

spirit of the spot maintains. It's a familiar story in the Emerald City: demolition for the sake of upward construction. With any luck, though, Seattle food lovers will get something even better in return.

In the meantime, Fremont's loss is Downtown's gain with Yang's Revel 1.5 pop-up, and if the chef has anything to say about it, the best is yet to come. "When our cooks go to other restaurants to eat or drink and they tell the bartenders they're from Revel, people always get happy," Yang muses. "They say, 'Oh my gosh! I love that place!' and that's really awesome to hear."

513 Westlake Ave. N
(206) 547-2040
relayrestaurantgroup.com/restaurants/revel/

YOROSHIKU

One of Seattle's best independent ramen restaurants almost never came to be. Before Keisuke Kobayashi ever dreamed of opening his Wallingford hot spot, he was an international student in Seattle working as an electrician. When his time in the States was up, he went home to take care of his sick mother, but after she passed, he wanted to move back to Seattle. A visa for an electrician, however, was impossible, but a visa for a Japanese restaurateur was possible.

"So, I started apprenticing in my hometown of Sapporo in a yakitori restaurant when I was thirty-two," Kobayashi says. "At that time, the Sapporo economy was so bad nobody would hire someone with no experience after the age of thirty. I told them I didn't need money. I just needed knowledge, technique. So I worked for over a year, and then I moved to America."

Kobayashi opened Yoroshiku in 2011, selling mostly yakitori skewers, but the customers loved the ramen he also had on the menu, and so he quickly adapted. But what does good ramen have that other variations don't? "It has to be made from scratch, for sure," says Kobayashi, who recently expanded his restaurant, "and it should have a style—tonkotsu, Southern Japanese, Sapporo. Also important is the soup temperature. Most American ramen restaurants make it warm, but here we make it hot."

While Kobayashi has several flavors of ramen on his menu, perhaps the best is the spicy miso ramen, served with a cooked egg that, if you let sit, will liquefy in the yolk center. If you ask Kobayashi, there is a right way and a wrong way to eat the delicious soup. "First, you taste the broth," he explains. "Second, you slurp the noodles. Don't eat

> "I started apprenticing in my hometown of Sapporo in a yakitori restaurant when I was thirty-two," Kobayashi says.

The art of ramen making is a world of technique and practice. Add a few trade secrets and you have Yoroshiku.

them . . . slurp. This is important. Slurping makes you eat the noodles with air, and you can taste more flavor. After that, taste the broth with the other ingredients, the bamboo, scallions, chashu."

Kobayashi's is not the only Japanese restaurant in the Wallingford neighborhood, which includes sushi spots and other ramen businesses, but it is likely the best, and it's this community of like-minded chefs that, in part, brought him to the neighborhood. "I like to compete," Kobayashi smiles. "I have confidence," and it shows. The warmth and skill in each bowl he serves is evident, and whether you're slurping or chewing, Kobayashi's ramen is the perfect comfort food on a gray, rainy Seattle day—of which there are many.

1911 N Forty-Fifth St.
(206) 547-4649
yoroshikuseattle.com

JUNEBABY

Seattle's Ravenna neighborhood is quiet and sleepy. Located in a sort of in-between area of the city, north of the bustling University District, south of Northgate Mall, and east of Green Lake, Ravenna has been a secret spot to live for a long time, but that is rapidly changing. With a light rail station in development, proposed sky-scraping apartment buildings, and two new restaurants from star Seattle chef Edouardo Jordan, there is much room to grow.

Jordan, who opened his first Ravenna restaurant, Salare, in 2015, opened his second Ravenna spot, JuneBaby, in 2017. "I think the easiest description is that Salare is my culinary journey, and JuneBaby is my history," muses Jordan, a James Beard–nominated chef. Salare's aesthetic is clean, bright, chic. Its menu, which includes items from Salare's garden, is the same. The vibe feels like how precise a young chef must be—crisp, knives sharpened, alert. JuneBaby, on the other hand, has roots in the soil. "It just made sense to do something that included what I love doing, what I love eating," Jordan says. "I kept going back to ideas of grilled and smoked meats, barbecue time with my dad, my grandmother's cooking."

So JuneBaby, which in 2018 won a James Beard Award for best new restaurant, became soul food. But soul food, or Southern food, Jordan says, has been represented too often by only one type of person and not enough by people of color, whose ancestors invented soul food during times of trouble and necessity. "It became somewhat of a calling," he says, "almost a mission to be that beacon, to be that chef that has the opportunity to present Southern food at its ultimate delight, from

Chef-owner Edouardo Jordan recently won two prestigious James Beard Awards for Best New Restaurant and Best Chef: Northwest.

JuneBaby exudes both elegance and soul, exemplified by this turkey leg braised in oxtail fat and then deep fried.

my point of view, that chef-of-color point of view. We look at the landscape of Southern food, and it's a story often told by white men, and there's nothing wrong with that, but the reality is that soul food and Southern food started by the hands of African slaves."

Jordan remembers his childhood, during which he and his family had to make do with what they had—not necessarily what he wanted. "At times," he says, "we didn't have the money to buy a fillet of anything, so we ate ox tails and pig tails and head cheese."

Today, JuneBaby's menu offers buttermilk biscuits, cast-iron cornbread, charred okra, crispy pig ear, smoked carrots, fried catfish, "Momma Jordan's Oxtails" made with turnips and pole beans, and shrimp gumbo. "Southern food was cooked by necessity, and those were the cuts I grew up on," Jordan says, "because that's what my mother was taught by her mom and what her mom was taught by my great-grandmother."

2122 NE Sixty-Fifth St.
(206) 257-4470
junebabyseattle.com

ZIPPY'S GIANT BURGERS

When owner Blaine Cook decided to open his classic Americana joint, Zippy's Giant Burgers, he went through many iterations of the menu's delicious burgers. He wanted to get things right. "At that point in time, we were trying to decide what kind of meat we would use for the hamburgers," Cook explains. "We went through a whole lot of different samples, and we just weren't digging them."

So Cook, for many years, decided to skip the middleman and ensure Zippy's ground its own meat for their meals, but, more recently, Cook says Zippy's has found the perfect partner, Double R Ranch, and this synergy has proven even more beneficial for his burgeoning eatery. Zippy's, which will continue to use 100 percent ground chuck beef and upward of two thousand pounds of it per week, won't miss a step, he says. Because of this confidence, Cook notes that his burger joint doesn't exactly serve hamburgers. "Instead," he says, "we serve hamburger sandwiches!"

Either way, what Zippy's, founded in 2008 and now with two locations—one in the Georgetown neighborhood and one in White Center—serves is delicious. The menu is a result of both experimentation and borrowing things from other menus Cook has come across. He says he and his family went though about ten different recipes for their black bean burger and eight to ten versions of their burger's "secret sauce." "We asked our friends," he says, "if you were to order a bacon cheeseburger, would you want the bacon on top of the cheese, underneath the cheese? Do you want your tomato on top of the burger or underneath?"

Zippy's Crown Burger, though, was inspired by a burger joint in the Midwest and at Zippy's, it's served with the secret sauce, a burger patty, pastrami, Swiss cheese, and locally made bread and butter pickles. Other menu items include the Great Dane burger, with Danish blue cheese; the Jimbo, with house-made pepper jack cheese and picked

Whether the burger is served on a big bun or sliced up into a salad, Zippy's delicious patties are where it's at.

jalapeños; and the Last Gasp, with hot links, a fried egg, bacon, and extra cheese. Also on the menu are Zippy's "vintage sodas" made with real sugar and, as a bonus for families, children eat free on Wednesdays.

For Cook, the community is an important aspect of his family-owned business. "We became part of the neighborhood," he says. "We have customers that used to come to our original location in Highland Park that still visit us today. Moms and dads would come in with their babies when we opened. Now their kids are nine or ten. That's the biggest satisfaction. The amount of community support has been really overwhelming."

9614 Fourteenth Ave. SW
(206) 763-1347
zippysgiantburgers.com

SAFECO FIELD

For Steve Dominguez, general manager of Centerplate, the organization responsible for the food and beverage operations at Seattle's professional baseball stadium, Safeco Field, the key to a great ballpark dining experience first begins with the aromas in the air. "For me," the seven-year veteran of Safeco says, "when I'm walking around, it starts not with a visual but a sense of smell. Is there popcorn, onions on the grill, meat going? The fresh cut grass is out there as well. There's an aroma to a good ballpark, and I feel we have that here."

While there are thirty Major League Baseball teams, few, if any, have a stadium concessionaire as focused on the high quality of food and beverage. In a city that has adopted craft and farm-to-table philosophies, those mantras have seeped into the stadium as well. "This is my seventh season with the Seattle Mariners," Dominguez explains, "but it's my twenty-fifth in baseball, and in almost every other ballpark it's dominated by American-style domestic light lagers." When he came out here, however, the focus was on IPAs and those beers that feature the lovely Yakima Valley hops. "There is a very educated consumer out here in Seattle," Dominguez says.

It doesn't stop with beer. Food is a major part of the Emerald City ecosystem as well. "Our position at Safeco," Dominguez explains, "is that we want to be judged along with every other streetside restaurant in Seattle." This philosophy was cemented in 2011, Dominguez says, when the stadium partnered with local chef/entrepreneur Ethan Stowell to bring in higher-quality, more nuanced eats made from locally sourced ingredients, such as Draper Valley chicken and Beecher's cheese. In fact, Dominguez's team is so willing to go out on a limb for the food at the ballpark that they brought in Oaxaca-style fried crickets. "Honestly," Dominguez says, "I didn't think we'd sell one order. More for us, not to be gimmicky, but to be authentic, but now we sell them all the time. They're a great topper for our soft tacos."

Seattle's professional baseball stadium takes such care with its food and beverages that fans are treated to delicious dumplings from the world-renowned Din Tai Fung.

One of the popular locations to grab a snack—whether that's a burger, cheese steak, or slice of pizza—is by the open-air bullpen (where the team's pitchers warm up). "It's a great social food and beverage space," Dominguez says. Another hot spot is the centerfield beer garden, where fans can get a drink and hope for a homerun hit to the gathering crowd.

In the end, though, for Dominguez, the key to a great ballpark experience is the standards: peanuts, popcorn, Cracker Jacks, and hot dogs—well, maybe bacon-wrapped hot dogs and even a crab sandwich. "Baseball is a grazing sport," he says. "Games can be six or even eight hours long. People are coming in to experience an entire ballpark. We want to make sure there is something for them on every level."

1250 First Ave. S
(206) 346-4001
mlb.com/mariners/

PECOS PIT BAR-B-QUE

When you've been around since 1980, it might be time to think about expanding, and that's exactly what this long-standing Seattle barbecue restaurant is planning to do. "We want to grow this thing across the country eventually," says Jeremy McLachlan, director of food and beverage with the company. "There's a trend we're starting to see with barbecue. It's not a fad slowing down and trailing off."

Barbecue has many styles and many subsections of fare, from Tennessee versions to Carolina to Texas, from ribs to brisket to chili mac, but at Pecos, the must-haves are the sandwiches. "Most barbecue places," says McLachlan, "think platters with white bread, but we're focused on a nice, hot, beautiful sandwich, and they should be deliciously sloppy."

One key to a good barbecue sandwich, he says, is to get the sauce on your fingers and in the corners of your mouth. Other important aspects include the toppings and the bun. "A softer bun is the way to go," notes McLachlan, who's been with the company five years. "You want the showpiece to be the meat, not the bun, but then the bun should hold up to it." Some toppings Pecos adds to its sandwiches are bacon, onions, and a beef hotlink they call a "spike." "And the sauce is everything," McLachlan says. "We serve it mild, medium, or hot, but it's all built on the base sauce. Ours has a big black pepper flavor with lots of great spice."

Another key is the wood used to smoke the meats. To the layperson, this may not seem important, but to the expert, it's paramount. Pecos,

> "Most barbecue places," says McLachlan, "think platters with white bread, but we're focused on a nice, hot, beautiful sandwich."

Pecos specializes in BBQ sandwiches, but try their signature chili Frito pie right out of the bag!

McLachlan says, uses 100 percent alder wood. "Alder has more of a soft smoke to it," he explains. "Not harsh like hickory or apple or cherry. Those have a high smoke. Alder doesn't give you heartburn."

Pecos, which began nearly forty years ago, now has two locations—one in the SoDo neighborhood and one in West Seattle—but McLachlan says they'd like to take the thing national. Why? Because, if for no other reason, barbecue is delicious and fun for the entire family. "I think making barbecue an everyday food for people is the biggest motivation," he says. "There's the old saying, 'You go to the restaurant for the food, but you come back because of the service.' At Pecos, we want you to walk in the door and have a good time."

2260 First Ave. S
(206) 623-0629
pecospit.com/sodo/

ODDFELLOWS CAFE + BAR

Owner Linda Derschang likes variety. It's why she travels as often as she can to pick up inspirations from other towns and cities and jaunts to bring back to Seattle and her half-dozen restaurants. At her all-day, all-night neighborhood café, Derschang has curated a place where people can come in for breakfast and grab a bowl of oatmeal or stay working on their computer through the night, sipping an elegant cocktail.

"I wanted to create my favorite neighborhood café that I hoped many other people would enjoy," Derschang says. "I wanted it to very much be a place where you could go by yourself to have breakfast, lunch, or dinner. Or a place where you could come with a small group of friends or a very large group."

To provide for such versatility, Oddfellows is equipped with a long, sixteen-person wooden table, like something out of a Nordic dining hall, and perhaps it is, since Oddfellows uses salvaged, recycled, or repurposed furnishings to make up its aesthetic. "It's a combination of loving beautiful, old things that you can't necessarily replicate today," Derschang says, "and it's an old building, and I wanted to give it a sense of history. Also, being sustainable is important."

The purpose, Derschang says, is for Oddfellows to be a place where you can ease in and do your own thing, and even better if a weary traveler—perhaps one like Derschang herself when she roams the world—strolls in to take a load off. "When you're traveling, you're frequently out tromping around a museum or shopping or sightseeing," she says. "I was just envisioning a place where someone could drop in and relax."

The menu for Oddfellows, says Derschang, couldn't be too dressy or precious or fancy. "And it was very important to me that we use local ingredients," she says. Standout items include the rich brioche French toast with mascarpone for brunch, the light English pea risotto for dinner, and the savory deviled eggs with capers for

Serving food from the decadent to the garden fresh, this European-inspired restaurant leaves you feeling fulfilled after each course. Photo credit: Morgen Schuler

happy hour.

While Oddfellows, which was established in 2008, is a local favorite, Derschang says she looks forward to what the new diners moving to the Emerald City will have to say about it. "A lot of people are moving to Seattle that are coming from larger cities," she says. "It's upping the level of sophistication in a really positive way. New people are embracing the cool food scene that we have in Seattle."

1525 Tenth Ave.
(206) 325-0807
oddfellowscafe.com

BANANAS GRILL

Seattle's Columbia City neighborhood is one of the city's most rapidly changing. In a city with seemingly more cranes than buildings across the skyline, it's Seattle's South End areas, traditionally inhabited by those of lower income, that are feeling the most pressure, and Columbia City, located right on the popular light rail station, is no exception. It's folks like Fowzi Abdi, owner of the Grill, who are working to keep good, affordable food in the area while offering a menu that's as diverse as the backgrounds of the people coming in to order from it.

People of all types frequent his restaurant, which Abdi calls "Mediterranean fast food." "I was looking for the right location ever since 2005," says the Somali native, who opened the eatery on November 11, 2011 (11/11/11). "The location mattered. I wanted to stay in South Seattle. I wanted to serve the community in that area." Abdi says he knows there are people of all income levels who eat at his establishment. "It feels like a place where people come together," he says, "and that's really great."

The Bananas Grill menu includes traditional hamburgers as well as a Hawaiian burger and a gyro burger; chicken shawarma, which, Abdi says, is "a lot of people's favorite plate"; samosas; and an array of dips and salads (including a falafel salsa). "People want their food fast," Abdi says. "So we keep everything fresh and simple as possible so we can get it to them as quickly as possible."

Simplicity is important when you're dealing with dishes from different regions and serving folks of all ages, backgrounds, family size, and income. There is little time and room to fiddle around if

"The location mattered," Abdi says. "I wanted to stay in South Seattle. I wanted to serve the community in that area."

Come into Bananas Grill and enjoy a fresh plate of salad, dip, pita bread, lamb, and rice. Healthy and fast dining!

you're trying to satisfy the taste buds of so many. "Columbia City is a vibrant place," Abdi offers. "It's one of the most diverse ZIP codes in the United States. People do talk about the cost of living going up, though, and people being displaced, which is very difficult, but overall, the neighborhood still has a great feel, and it's growing."

Abdi remembers seeing his restaurant filled to capacity on Eid al-Fitr, which is the final day of Ramadan, the religious month of fasting observed by Muslims. "People all scooted together," Abdi smiles. "It was awesome. All kinds of people were getting together who didn't know each other, and that's what makes a community."

4556 Martin Luther King Jr. Way S
(206) 420-4839
bananasgrillseattlewa.com

RAY'S BOATHOUSE

If nothing else, the people behind the restaurant Ray's Boathouse want you to have a connection with Puget Sound. "Both the space and the menu," says Douglas Zellers, co-owner and general manager of Ray's, "are created to connect our guests to the water. Everything we source, from the way we present our dishes to the view from the tables, is about creating a deep connection with the waterfront."

Ray's, Zellers says, which overlooks Shilshole Bay in the city's western Ballard neighborhood, began first from a modest boat rental shop in 1939 owned by a fellow named Ray. That shop turned into a little café, which eventually sold fish and chips (while still renting boats). The business blossomed into a "real" restaurant and was later sold in 1973.

Zellers, who came on as general manger in 2012, says from those humble beginnings, classic Northwest cuisine was born. "There was no Northwest cuisine before," Zellers says. "The owners [in 1973] had an immense desire to take local products, primarily from the sea, and cook them in their perfect state and present them to guests with very little meddling around."

As the recent history of seafood unfolded, Zellers says Ray's was at the forefront of ocean-to-table movements, including working with Bruce Gore. A commercial fisherman, Gore pioneered the "frozen at sea" fishing technique, in which fish are frozen right after they are caught to freeze them to preserve them in their freshest possible state. "We take these amazing animals and just don't mess with it," Zellers says.

A spectacle to look at, Ray's constitutes two main dining areas. The upstairs café area, with a large deck overhanging the water, serves lunch and dinner. The downstairs restaurant is more fine dining and is only open for dinner. Much of the fish Ray's uses for its immaculate dishes comes from Alaska. "We work primarily direct

With a stunning view and an epic menu, Ray's is quintessential Seattle dining, especially if you love fresh seafood. Photo credit: Morgen Schuler

with fishermen," Zellers says. "Most of the fish is sourced from cold waters of the Northwest," including salmon from the Columbia River andhalibut moving north from Washington to Alaska. "The best fish come from the waters off of Neah Bay, the northwestmost portion of the state on the peninsula." The shellfish, he says, come from Puget Sound: mussels, clams, oysters.

The most popular dishes, Zellers explains, are the Pacific sablefish in sake kasu (black cod soaked in sake lees), the fresh-caught wild salmon, and halibut. "That's the big three," he says. "With our dishes, there's no doctoring it up. We want the essence of the seafood to shine. No sauces to cover it up or heavy cooking techniques. Just the freshest possible seafood."

6049 Seaview Ave. NW
(206) 789-3770
rays.com

LE PICHET (AND CAFÉ PRESSE)

The things we do as youngsters are often what we're meant to do as adults, and while Jim Drohman, co-owner of the Seattle French restaurants Le Pichet and Café Presse, went to work for local engineering company Boeing for a handful of years, it was really the experience of cooking, which he'd started at age fifteen, that led him to his life's work.

"I put myself through college as a line cook," Drohman says. "Then, after being at Boeing for five years, I decided it was not for me. My wife and I moved to Paris. I did my culinary training at a French public vocational high school." He chose France because the origin of fine dining seems to always point back to there. "I worked in Paris for two years, then I came back to Seattle."

Drohman opened Le Pichet downtown in 2000 because, he says, "at that time a simple, family-run regional traditional restaurant that we loved so much in Paris was missing in Seattle." Drohman wanted to create French-style restaurants outside the vein of what most people think of as French dining: stuffy, snooty, expensive, and not for them. "If you've been to France, you know that's a small percentage," he says. "Most people's dining experience is in a simple restaurant likely never to get a Michelin star."

With the background in engineering, Drohman's training to think logically helps in his in business. "It's all about organization and working in a way that's logical," he notes, and in 2007 he made the logical step to open Café Presse in Seattle's Capitol Hill neighborhood. "We finally decided to take the plunge." So, Drohman opened what he calls a "bar-café," something he saw much of in France. "In Paris," he says, "if you're going to meet friends, you don't go to a bar across town. You go to the place on the corner. It's like a multipurpose room in your neighborhood."

Inspired by the light French family lunches that can go on for hours and hours with multiple courses, Café Presse is fit for any group. Photo credit: Morgen Schuler

While the menus for the two restaurants both work with the same philosophy—from scratch and using seasonal ingredients—Drohman says the aesthetic at Café Presse is "a little simpler, a little younger, modern in the sense that the food is from the last fifty years instead of the last hundred." At Le Pichet, you can order meats and cheeses, chicken liver, pâté, and braised pork cheeks, all while feeling like you're being served from a delicate but masterful chef. At Café Presse, there are omelets, croque-monsieurs, and pork-duck sausage. "I love to go to places and see regional food," Drohman says, "to see how a dish happened. I find that endlessly fascinating."

1933 First Ave.
(206) 256-1499
lepichetseattle.com

THE ANGRY BEAVER

Tim Pipes, owner and founder of Greenwood's favorite hockey bar, has had some bad luck. He's endured a National Hockey League player strike, a gas explosion to a nearby business that shut his place down, and, on the personal side of things, a dramatic divorce. Nevertheless, over the past five years, his Angry Beaver Bar has subsisted, serving drinks and bar fare to eager hockey fans.

Pipes, who had worked a handful of jobs before opening his bar, including a stint working with Apple technologies, became sick of the corporate world. He found himself at forty-eight years old wondering what he was going to do with the rest of his life. At that time, he moved back to his native Canada (Pipes is from Toronto) and fell in love with hockey culture all over again. "The Maple Leafs were on every screen in every bar," says Pipes. "People were out skating on ponds, buddies were getting together at arenas. When I came back to Seattle, I was having a hell of a time finding a place to watch it. I was usually relegated to the smallest TV with the sound off."

In addition to the sport, Pipes says he wanted to make a place that was Canadian friendly, which includes serving Canada's favorite food: poutine. "The majority of what I sell is poutine," he says. "Really, we are a Canadian-themed hockey bar. We did Canadian Thanksgiving on October 9, and we opened up the shop for the gold-medal game between Sweden and Canada at 3:00 a.m."

The Angry Beaver serves traditional poutine with local Beecher's cheese curds and house-made beef gravy, or you can get it with mushroom or turkey gravy. And while poutine is the regulars' favorite, hungry hockey fans can also order a traditional peameal bacon sandwich, a flank steak sandwich, or a French dip, among other options. "The ultimate poutine is when you have the fries and you crumble cheese on top, then pour the gravy," Pipes muses. "You get the cheese melting down through the French fries. By the time

While customers watch hockey games, they can savor big plates of burgers hot off the grill, best when paired with poutine gravy fries.

it hits your table, you have this crispy, chewy mess. It's the perfect bar food."

What might work best for Pipes, however, is that Seattle, a city of many transplants, makes for a good clientele for a bar with many televisions featuring games from cities all across North America. "When the Chicago Blackhawks are playing, I'll see fifty Blackhawk jerseys," Pipes notes. "Same with the Leafs, the San Jose Sharks, LA Kings, Detroit, Pittsburgh. It's a city of transplants. A lot of people that were starved now have their home sport acknowledged in Seattle."

8412 Greenwood Ave. N
(206) 782-6044
angrybeaverseattle.com

SHORTY'S

Shorty's, the twenty-plus-year-old historic pinball arcade in Seattle's Belltown neighborhood, is in a tough spot. As the city continues to grow and change, the threat looms over all the businesses sharing the block with Shorty's: they could be demolished at any time.

Yet, the place remains. It is a beacon to those who love to socialize around a game of pinball. While Shorty's is owned and operated by Avout Vander Werf, it was his ex-wife who opened the business in 1997. When she decided to move on, Vander Werf, who'd worked for decades fixing and restoring pinball machines, took it over. "I was always interested in pinball, even as a little kid," says Vander Werf. "A pinball machine is a very unique product. It's sitting right there on the intersection of art, wizardry, engineering, and salesmanship."

Buildings around Shorty's have, at times, received landmark status, a boon to those businesses, perhaps even preserving them into the future. But the threat of condos and new construction hangs heavy over the businesses that have yet to be so lucky. "I don't know how much longer Shorty's will be here," sighs Vander Werf. Nevertheless, he remains hopeful. "I don't know if my building is ever going to see landmark status, but maybe there is a different way to preserve it," he muses. "It's the living room for a lot of people who live in Belltown and a destination for many more people."

While the arcade games and the carnival feel of the place bring a lot of folks through the doors, it's also the kitschy appreciation of Shorty's hot dog menu that many find tantalizing. "I personally prefer a hot dog with everything: kraut, relish, onions, mustard, and ketchup, but we have everything from naked to chili cheese." Other menu items include a Vegi Bigtop with vegetarian chili cheese sauce; a Chicago Style Dog with a sweet pickle, mustard, relish, onions, peppers, tomatoes, and celery salt; and the Number 3 with tomatoes, cream cheese, and local Mama Lil's peppers.

The front door of Shorty's is as iconic in the Emerald City as the sound of a ringing pinball machine.

The boardwalk feel permeates Shorty's, from the smell of the hot dogs to the clinking of drinking glasses to the arcade games. "We were offering pinball before it was hip," remarks Vander Werf. "Pinball was kind of dying at one point, but ever since then it's made a big comeback, and it basically started here in the Pacific Northwest. Yet, if everybody walked away and said they were tired of it, we'd still be doing it. It's just what we do."

2222 Second Ave.
(206) 441-5449
shortydog.com

PROLETARIAT PIZZA

"We'd never done this before," says Stefanie Albaeck, who along with her husband, Mike, opened the White Center pizzeria in 2009. "We had never made a pizza!" But the couple received their first test when a cured meats distributor brought some product to the shop they were building up for an as-yet-unnamed restaurant and said the best way to test the stuff was on a cooked pizza. So, the couple dove in headfirst.

In the years between, the couple has created one of the best and most welcoming pizzerias in the Emerald City. For a city not known for its pizza pies, Proletariat is a stellar option not just for Seattle but for any city, which is good because, as Mike says, "We didn't want to be doing what we were previously doing before Proletariat."

Parents of two children, Mike, who worked in telecommunications, and Stefanie, who worked as a hair stylist, wanted to open a business where their children could be around them. So, they created the family-friendly restaurant complete with arcade games and a photo booth, but that doesn't mean the couple had any strong clue of what they were doing at the onset. "To be completely honest," says Mike, "we didn't decide on the idea ourselves in a way. I began talking with Justin, who owns Full Tilt Ice Cream across the street, and he said, 'Every neighborhood needs a pizza place,' and as we thought about it more, we decided to do it."

Proletariat's pizza, served as a pie or by the slice, is made on the thinner side of the spectrum and includes fresh ingredients. "We wanted to make a pizza that we wanted to eat," says Stefanie. "So I began cold calling vendors asking them if they sold the right kind of mozzarella. At the time, we didn't have much to lose. We started Proletariat on an extreme shoestring budget. We were winging it."

The surrounding neighborhood has embraced them so much that they've "forgiven all our mistakes," says Mike. "People were so

The inventive dough slingers at Proletariat are always thinking about new toppings that might blow your mind. Photo credit: Morgen Schuler

glad we moved into the neighborhood. They were willing to figure it out with us." Standout menu items include the sausage pie with fresh chopped garlic and local Mama Lil's peppers; the traditional margarita; and the house specialty, the ham and egg pizza, which is only served as a whole pie. "When we started," Mike adds, "we had no experience whatsoever, but we decided to give it a shot," and now they are on the brink of ten years. "It's amazing," he says. "We love it!"

9622 Sixteenth Ave. SW
(206) 432-9765
proletariatpizza.com

THE RICKSHAW

Located in the northern Shoreline neighborhood of the city, the Rickshaw is both old and weird. It's a time capsule that its patrons investigate on a daily basis. What began as a pancake house in the late fifties later became the Rickshaw in the mid-seventies, and now the place is a fabled, rickety, and beloved home for American Chinese food, cheap stiff drinks, and karaoke seven nights a week.

"When I bought it," says current owner Hong Li, who purchased the Rickshaw in 2013, "I was looking for a restaurant, but I didn't have any experience owning one in the United States. That was, I don't want to say a mistake, but a lesson." It turns out for Li, who owned two bars in China before moving to America to get married (she's since divorced), that that was the first of many lessons. She soon began to learn about her clientele: local people who like to drink, eat, and sing. "People act differently when they have a drink," remarks Li. "Also, I think people don't want to stay at home by themselves. They want to come to a space and talk or spend time with other people."

Indeed, more than a sit-down restaurant, the Rickshaw is a place for people to let their weird out over a plate of orange chicken and a gin and tonic. "People come by and treat here like it's their home," Li says. "This is their social life," and a lot of those people have been spending their money at the Rickshaw for decades. "We have a lot of old people as our neighbors," she says. "Rickshaw is probably the oldest Chinese-American restaurant in the Seattle area. So there are many people who still remember this place because they probably had a meal here when they were younger."

While the menu hasn't changed much in nearly forty years—think General Tso chicken, chop suey—Li also hasn't changed much of the architecture, furniture, or ambiance. Even as the rent for the place

This classic Northwest dive crossed with a comfort food Chinese restaurant will have you singing into the night with its seven-nights-a-week karaoke jams.

has increased from its original one hundred dollars per month to its current eight thousand, the interior is virtually the same, much to the appreciation of the Rickshaw's customers. "I did a little bit of updates, and we got a lot of regulars complaining," she laughs, "but it's too old!"

Yet, the people keep venturing in to sing and eat. "I think everybody," Li muses, "sometimes they have a drink, and they can think they are a movie star. They could be standing on stage performing, and there's an audience. With a karaoke party, it can be that way."

322 N 105th St.
(206) 789-0120
seattlerickshaw.com

SALUMI ARTISAN CURED MEATS

With an old-world sensibility not often found in contemporary brick-and-mortars, Salumi, founded in 1999, caters to folks who want something very particular: cured meats. What started as a retirement project for Armandino Batali after thirty-one years working at Boeing has turned into a beloved hot spot for salamis, sandwiches, and muscle meats such as legs and bellies.

To cure a specific cut can take anywhere between one month and nine, says Salumi co-owner Gina Batali (if the last name sounds familiar, she is the sister of New York chef/entrepreneur Mario Batali). "Proper curing relies on many factors," she says. "One is time. Another is diameter." While Batali and her staff don't butcher any animals, they do trim cuts, say, the jowls, for proper curing. The meats are then dry rubbed with salt and spices, put into tubs, taken out and cleaned, rubbed again, put back into the tub, and then hung for one or several months. For salamis, the meat is ground, mixed with the proper ratio of fats and spices, tied, fermented in an oven, and hung for a month or so.

Batali, who left a career in the corporate world of General Electric to help take over her family business, says her shop, which includes an on-site deli, wholesale distribution, and a sandwich shop, sources meats from farms all over the country, and Seattleites come from all over the city to stand in line during lunch hours for Salumi's famous sandwiches, which range from gooey meatball and savory porchetta to a plethora of options utilizing their salamis.

It's not just folks from the Emerald City venturing to get a taste of the meaty wares. "Phil Cuzzi," says Batali, "he's an umpire for Major League Baseball. He comes by when the league assigns him to Seattle, and he sends other umpires here as well. He's got

A hearty sandwich is but one of the many treats you're in store for at this longtime cured meat hot spot.

this total Philly/New Jersey accent. Sometimes he jumps on the sandwich line. He bikes here from his hotel wearing this Salumi shirt we gave him, like, seven years ago. The staff just loves him. Those are the people that make it."

Indeed, for Batali, more than her expertly cured and packaged salami and muscle meats, it's the people she encounters that make the experience of owning and operating Salumi rich, which even includes bringing on new, enthusiastic business partners Clara Veniard and Martinique Grigg, as the restaurant did this year. No matter who is in this shop, the eatery will always feel like a family affair. "Taking over the business," she says, "was a chance to work with my parents and a chance for our children to be with their grandparents. It's been really nice to come back home."

309 Third Ave. S
(206) 621-8772
salumicuredmeats.com

HONEYHOLE SANDWICHES

"**A** sandwich has to be well executed," says Sean London, founder of Capitol Hill's HoneyHole. "Not just slapped together. A sandwich comes in many different forms. It seems like a really simple concept, but you have to work at all aspects of the sandwich to make the complete package."

London, who started his sit-down sandwich shop in 1999 with his brother, Devon, and now co-owns it with business partner Hannah Roberts, says when he moved to Seattle in 1996 that there were no great sandwich options, and as someone who loves the handheld delights, this was a big problem. "We thought something special could be created," London notes.

He and his brother were right. The HoneyHole, whose name is derived from an old fisherman's term meaning a "secret spot" plentiful with fish, is regarded as one of the city's best sandwich stops, if not its premier version. "It starts with really good bread," London offers, "and then well-cooked, properly seasoned meat, cheese, and fresh produce, and, of course, high-quality condiments."

London recalls one night making his own sandwich from HoneyHole leftovers. "I had some of our smoked brisket in my fridge, and I ended up sautéing it in its own smoky fat with onions and peppers," he says. "I served it up on a nice, hot baguette with melted pepper jack cheese. It was insanely good. Simple but full of flavor."

It's the simplicity that London emphasizes when he talks sandwiches in general. He says the sandwich, much like the idea of pizza, is malleable, and everyone has their own version of it

> "It starts with really good bread," London offers, "and then well-cooked, properly seasoned meat, cheese, and fresh produce, and, of course, high-quality condiments."

Gooey, oh-so-tasty sandwich with a creamy side of potato salad and a tiny planted flag.

despite its simple recipe and components. Some of HoneyHole's top choices include the Fast Eddie, with house-roasted tri-tip; the Wave Rider, with roasted turkey, pesto, and smoked Gouda; and the hot vegetarian Bellissimo with smoked field roast and red pepper mayo. "We were one of the first sandwich places in Seattle to really focus on oven-roasted hot sandwiches," London says, and HoneyHole has an extensive menu of them, including many vegetarian, vegan, and gluten-free options.

While the burgeoning Capitol Hill neighborhood around HoneyHole always changes, the restaurant itself, London says, is also continually evolving. "When we opened in 1999," he says, "it was a tight-knit neighborhood, almost like a unique little microeconomy. Everyone lived and worked in the neighborhood. As far as our place changing, we've always been working on in-house operations to run a better restaurant, to make it more efficient, to make it a better place for our employees, which, ultimately, is about making it a more unique experience for our customers."

703 E Pike St.
(206) 709-1399
thehoneyhole.com

DUKE'S SEAFOOD & CHOWDER

If one thing's for sure about restaurant owner Duke Moscrip, it's that he cares vigorously about seafood. It's why he left a career in a brokerage firm and started working in the restaurant business in the seventies, starting Ray's Boathouse in 1972 and eventually founding Duke's—which now has upward of seven locations throughout the city—on February 18, 1977. "We broke a lot of rules in those early days," Moscrip laughs. "We paid everybody in cash every night. We poured the best liquor in our well. We started serving wine by the glass, which had never been done before with good varietal wines."

One thing Duke's is famous for is its award-winning chowder, and Moscrip is not afraid to give out the secret. "The secret to chowder is the roux," he says, "the flour and the butter. You must cook that roux and get it to 175 degrees and cook it for seven to eight minutes at that temperature. Get it to 175 and keep it there! You can't put carrots in chowder, no peppers either."

Beyond caring passionately about his famous chowders, Moscrip warns of the "crisis" the country faces concerning seafood. "We have a problem," he says. "Our salmon are endangered. The Columbia River used to have fifteen to thirty million fish to spawn. Last year it was 457,000." As for seafood, sustainability at the source is paramount, he says. "I understand what it takes to get consistently great seafood every day," Moscrip explains. "I'm the only restaurant guy who fishes with the fishermen. You have to go there to figure it out."

While Duke's menu is about 90 percent seafood, it originally started out serving such items as veal, New York strips, and fish and chips. Now, though, things are honed, clearer of vision. "The fish have to be caught, iced, bled, filleted, and frozen below forty degrees

All Duke's cares about is catching, preserving, and serving the best seafood in the world. No big deal.

and vacuum packed," Moscrip explains. "There are very few places where you can get a good list of seafood that's really taken care of properly. You don't get good seafood by accident."

So to help grow and sustain the items that make up his menu at his seven locations—items such as coconut-encrusted prawns, Dungeness crab-stuffed halibut, and sea cod tacos, Moscrip has gotten political, writing an open letter to President Trump asking that he and the rest of the federal government look into better preservation practices, noting that with decreased salmon there is decreased revenue and decreased food sources. "I'm very proud of what we do," Moscrip says, "and every day we try to look to see how we can make it better."

901 Fairview Ave. N
(206) 382-9963
dukesseafood.com

FARESTART

Nearly every week, says FareStart marketing and communications director Stephanie Schoo, there is a new transformational moment with the FareStart program, which helps people enter the workforce after experiencing homelessness and poverty. At its flagship location on 700 Virginia Street in Seattle's downtown neighborhood last year, FareStart had 214 employment placements in its adult culinary program, and across all of its programs, it placed a total of 314 people.

"One of the highlights of working for FareStart," says Schoo, "happens on Thursday evenings. It's also our Guest Chef Night, where we bring in a well-known chef who prepares a three-course meal with our students. It's part fundraiser, and also it's a training opportunity. The graduates who come through our program graduate that night."

Schoo says seeing the "very brave people transform" after coming into the program and not knowing what to expect—after leaving prison or living in the streets—is very rewarding and hopeful. "It's pretty powerful," she says, "and it happens almost on a weekly basis. Ninety percent of our grads who come through the adult culinary program get a job within days or, at most, three months."

It's truly an astonishing success rate for the organization, which was started by David Lee. He originally found himself delivering meals to shelters and the folks living there, but soon, says Schoo, the efforts shifted to teaching students in one of FareStart's now-handful of locations in Beacon Hill, Rainier Valley, South Lake Union, and other neighborhoods.

FareStart, which started in 1992, Schoo says, offers a sense of community as well as training skills to its students. "Food nourishes the body and soul," she says, "and the restaurant industry in particular is very forgiving. It's not so much about your past as it is focused on what you're doing now and where you're going." The project itself is

This sunny-side-up egg polenta is just one of the many expertly created and stunningly appealing dishes from FareStart in Seattle.

growing, with the conglomerate Amazon recently donating twenty-five thousand square feet to FareStart for five new eateries.

Because there are so many FareStart locations throughout the city, from full-service restaurants to salad spots to cafés, there are many food options to try, even as you're helping out the people who share the city. "Seattle has changed," Schoo says, noting the recent climb in homelessness rates. "FareStart's apprenticeship program gives opportunities to folks to move forward in their careers, to scale up and get higher-level skills, and to get living-wage jobs after they leave the program. As long as homelessness seems to be a challenge in the city, FareStart will step up and do more."

700 Virginia St.
(206) 267-7601
farestart.org

FULL TILT ICE CREAM

When Justin Cline opened the first franchise for his soon-to-be expansive ice cream and pinball business, Full Tilt, he didn't think anyone would show up, not on the first day, anyway. But much to his surprise, and his wife's as well, some nine hundred people came, and the first day's batch of ice cream sold out completely.

"That's when my wife and I turned to each other and said, 'This is going to work. We're going to do this,'" says Cline. But Seattle—and ice cream—are fickle entities. "Then winter hit," laughs Cline. "Some days we'd make, like, fifteen dollars. We thought, 'Oh, crap, we're screwed,' but it's totally worked out. All the neighborhoods we're in have been so supportive."

Full Tilt, which opened its first shop in 2008 in the southerly White Center neighborhood, has become such an Emerald City institution that famed musical performers Mudhoney and Damien Jurado have played many shows on location, and people come from all around to get a few scoops, play pinball (a facet of the shop inspired, says Cline, by Shorty's in Belltown), and shop the store's comic books or candy.

"At the time," says Cline, who worked in restaurants in college but never with ice cream, "my wife was a teacher. We were going to a lot of community meetings. I wanted to open a storefront in the neighborhood. At the time, there weren't a lot of businesses in White Center. So I asked the community, and they said they wanted a bookstore, movie theater, or an ice cream shop. So, I said yes to ice cream!"

Since those first days, the ice cream options at Full Tilt, which now has five locations around the city, have grown and multiplied. Today, they include vegan chocolate orange chip (Cline's favorite), Thai iced tea, coffee Oreo and, yes, Mudhoney (named after the band). "Ice cream is actually really easy to do," says Cline, who adds that he'd never made a tub of ice cream until the day before he opened the shop, "and

The multicolored universe that is Full Tilt has put a sugary smile on the faces of countless customers. Photo credit: Morgen Schuler

everybody loves ice cream. When we started, I was a little scared. We didn't even have a business plan, but everyone's been so wonderful."

Beyond the ice cream, Full Tilt remains special because of the confluence of treasures within its walls, from sweets to superheroes. "Both my wife and I love pinball and geek culture," Cline says. "It just seemed like it would be a fun throwback where people could come hang out and not just get ice cream and leave, but they could hang out for a while, read, play games, and just enjoy themselves."

5041 Rainier Ave. S
(206) 226-2740
fulltilticecream.com

CAPITOL CIDER

When her son approached her with an idea about a new restaurant business, owner Julie Tall was smart to listen. Her son, seeing the rise in appreciation for craft beer throughout the Pacific Northwest, thought that craft cider would be the next hip trend to take off. "He accurately identified it," Tall recalls. "He pitched me the idea in 2010, and we opened our little place in 2012."

Capitol Cider, located in the heart of Seattle's Capitol Hill neighborhood, has become a favorite hot spot in the eclectic neighborhood. The place, which celebrated its fifth birthday in 2017, is also equipped with an expansive basement area, complete with eleven-foot ceilings that Tall redesigned, and has blossomed into one of the city's cutest and most appealing places to see art and performance. "Monday nights there's a jazz jam session," she says, "and Tuesday nights we have musical theater sing-a-long. Some of the people who come in know every single lyric to every single song! Thursdays we do drink and draw with a live model."

Along with all the options for enjoying the arts on-site, at Capitol Cider, patrons can order any number of the many craft ciders available, from tart berry options to über dry apple ciders to perries (ciders made entirely from pears). "In 2012," says Tall, "the yearly Cider Summit had like three hundred people attend. Now, there's like four thousand. Cider's popularity has grown astronomically." The bar and restaurant also offer an entirely gluten-free menu. "When we opened," Tall says, "we didn't tell people. We didn't advertise that for years. Being gluten free was a little known concept except for the people who really cared about it. Now, it's everywhere. Because of that, we've attracted people with lots of different food sensitivities."

Capitol Cider often hosts music in its subterranean bar, from open mics to high caliber jazz.

If you like cider (and goodness knows America's Founding Fathers did) then Capitol Cider is your watering hole. Photo credit: Morgen Schuler

Tall says she regularly works to pair the lunch and dinner menu items with ciders available on tap, and while craft cider is always increasing in popularity, Tall aims to underscore that it's also been around a long time. In this way, Capitol Cider is a bridge to the old and new drinking worlds. "Cider traditions are strong in France, Spain, England," she notes, "and America was raised on hard cider. If people's water wasn't potable, they would just ferment it and make hard cider."

818 E Pike St.
(206) 397-3564
capitolcider.com

PORTAGE BAY CAFE

Every once in a while owner John Gunnar doesn't mind a customer finding a happy little bug on a salad leaf. "There are the people who ask for a new salad," he says, "and then there are the people who scream and yell." Gunnar, whose popular and profitable cafés dot a handful of neighborhoods throughout the city, has been trading in organic food for about two decades. He knows that if a little slug likes the lettuce on the plate, that means it's real and healthy food. "You don't want to have food where there's no possibility of a slug landing on it," he says.

Founded in 1997, Portage Bay's original café was built in the Emerald City's Roosevelt neighborhood, and if you were to drive by on a weekend morning, you'd likely see a line out the door for hours on end. Inside, patrons sit at one of the many small breakfast tables in the large dining space. Friendly servers take orders and sling mugs of coffee and glasses of orange juice to morning diners. While the café bustles today with organic fare, it was originally started simply as a business. "We started the restaurant at that point just to make money," Gunnar says. "About three years later, we started getting into organics and really heavily emphasized farm-to-table in 2001. That's when we took off."

Menu items that draw the continuous crowds include an array of Benedicts, such as Dungeness crab cake, smoked salmon, pork belly, and shrimp and cornbread, as well as biscuits and gravy, myriad omelets, and a heaping breakfast bar teaming with French toast options and pancakes—dishes made with taste as well as sustainability and health in mind. Gunnar says that over the years he has become increasingly interested in food production, especially

> "You don't want to have food where there's no possibility of a slug landing on it," – John Gunnar

Specializing in classic breakfast fare, this long-standing Seattle eatery has served thousands of plates, including its scrumptious eggs Benedict. Photo credit: Morgen Schuler

when considering the power of humans to manipulate it. "I think it's very scary how smart we are," he says. "We have the ability to produce so much, but the problem is our food is often produced in such quick and poor ways with pesticides and herbicides that cause terrible environmental degradation. We've got to do something to change it."

One small way to change it is by reimagining the food system and including more and more sustainable and organic products, Gunnar notes. While cost and volume remain important factors in feeding a community, if the food is prepared well, healthy, and filling, people might be willing to pay a little more for it. "When we went into business," Gunnar says, "everybody did breakfast, but they all did it on the cheap. We thought instead of paying $4.99 for eggs, hash browns, toast, and coffee, we'd charge ten dollars and twelve dollars for the organic eggs and organic bread. I thought it would scare the heck out of people, but they showed up in droves."

391 Terry Ave. N
(206) 462-6400
portagebaycafe.com

LA ISLA

This Puerto Rican restaurant wants nothing more than for you to feel at home and comfortable, yet also transported, and to do so, they flood your five senses with Caribbean tastes, smells, sights, and sounds, from the bright colors on the walls to the fresh ingredients on the plates. The restaurant, born in a farmers market in 2004 from family recipes and family business partnerships, brings a lot from native Puerto Rico to the bustling Ballard neighborhood. "For us," says operating partner Vicente Bravo, "it's not just about selling food. We believe it's our duty to educate people about our culture and flavors."

Puerto Rican food, says Bravo, is a mixture of many heritages and cultures, from folks native to the island to Spanish, Italians, to Africans. Yet, transporting the flavors of the island to the small northwest corner of the United States is not an easy task all the time. "The biggest challenge we have," says Bravo, "is trying to copy the Caribbean cuisine with ingredients over here. It's tougher, but we're close." Certain ingredients, such as garlic, peppers, and tomatoes, are common, of course, but others, such as recao, which is like Mexican coriander, are very difficult to find.

When speaking about his restaurant, Bravo mentions aunts and cousins and his mother and grandmother. Indeed, the source of inspiration for the dishes, which include beef and chicken stews, cod-stuffed avocados, and deep-fried prawns, is truly a family affair. "People come in," he says, "who have never tried our food, and they say it's delicious, like it feels like their grandma's cuisine." Bravo compares it to American Southern fare. "It's our soul food," he says.

In fact, many of the recipes resemble family meals so much that some have their own personal origin stories. "When we were all kids," says Bravo, "our grandma would make a big pot of rice and beans for the whole family. My cousin who started the restaurant

An array of authenticity is displayed at the cozy La Isla eatery, from grilled salmon to fresh greens and red beans and rice.

was the pickiest eater back then. So our grandma would make a special batch just for him. Now, twenty years later, that's the recipe he uses at La Isla."

If that's not enough to lure you into the festive and sweet-smelling eatery, they have dozens and dozens of rums for making cocktails or sipping with dinner. "We are trying to make people realize they can drink rum with their dinner," the patriotic Bravo explains, "but it's all an education process, and that's why we're here."

2320 NW Market St.
(206) 789-0516
laislacuisine.com

LITTLE UNCLE

In a city rich with sparkling, white-tablecloth restaurants with elongated menus and head chefs with famous names, there are also those spots in the city many would call a hole-in-the-wall—eateries that are unassuming, small, born out of a concept that's formed during long nights in tiny kitchens. Places like Little Uncle. "If you talk to any restaurant owners," says co-owner Poncharee Kounpungchart, "they're all going to say that if you don't hustle, you're not going to last."

Poncharee and her husband, Wiley Frank, planted the seeds for Little Uncle in 2010. The spot started as a pop-up for a year, which included a season at the Columbia City farmers market. Eventually, Poncharee and Frank found a small one-hundred-square-foot location on Madison Street, which she called "the Hallway." These days they're still on Madison but in a bigger location. "It's really hard to get a space if you don't have a lot of money," admits Poncharee. "It can be hard to have anyone care about what you're doing, but now we've been on the same block for seven years. Can you believe it?"

Poncharee and Frank decided to try their hand at the restaurant business because they both loved food. While Poncharee didn't have much experience in the industry, her husband was a trained chef, and after a year in Thailand learning ingredients and working to build recipes, the two came back to America and began their endeavor. "We lived in Thailand for a year," says Poncharee, who was born in that country and moved to America when she was nine. "When we came back to the States, Wiley was asked to start

> "If you talk to any restaurant owners," says co-owner Poncharee Kounpungchart, "they're all going to say that if you don't hustle, you're not going to last."

Little Uncle owner Wiley Frank, admiring a few fresh plates in his cozy eatery.
Photo credit: Morgen Schuler

a pop-up. We thought it was a good idea to test the market and build a clientele. We kept moving from there."

Little Uncle's menu is compact, utilizing ingredients from both America and Thailand—the fresh stuff from the States and the authentic from Thailand. Says Poncharee, "It's only worth it if you crave it." The chefs compose the dishes if it's something they want to eat, she adds. Popular items include the phad thai (of course!); beef noodles with Chinese celery, fried garlic, and chili vinegar; and khao soi gai, or Chiang Mai chicken curry with egg noodles, coconut milk, and red curry paste. "We're bringing what we learned from Thailand to America," Poncharee says, "while keeping the flavors and ingredients fresh. There's only a few items on the menu. We want to minimize choices so we can control the top quality."

1523 E Madison St., #101
(206) 549-6507
littleuncleseattle.com

LA CARTA DE OAXACA

It's almost impossible to be a small, family-owned restaurant and survive Seattle's changing landscape and the eruption of cranes and condos all over the city skyline. It's probably that much harder to be a family not from the United States trying to navigate these hurdles and do it in Ballard, one of the Emerald City's most changed neighborhoods. Yet, La Carta de Oaxaca has managed a fifteen-year career in the city and even expanded to a second location in the Queen Anne neighborhood. How did they do it?

The secret is the strong sense of family, says Robert Dominguez, assistant manager at the restaurant as well as son of the owner and grandson of the head chef, Gloria Perez. "I have regulars come in," says Dominguez, twenty-one, who started at the restaurant at sixteen, "and it's gotten more to the point where they hug me instead of just saying hello. We've built a bond with our customers to the point where no matter what I think, we'll be okay."

The restaurant is born out of the family's history in in Oaxaca, a small state in southern Mexico separated from much of the surrounding land by mountains. The area, known for mole and spicy food, was home to Dominguez's father, who emigrated to the United States from a small town (about the size of Ballard, Dominguez says) called Santa Cruz Etla. La Carta de Oaxaca, which opened its doors in 2003 (and expanded to Queen Anne in 2013), celebrates this region with its house special mole sauce, made by Dominguez's grandmother. "Mole is a very traditional sauce in Oaxaca," he says. "It varies by region. The way my grandmother knows how to cook it is sweet. She is the only one who knows how to make it. I would never try it."

Signature dishes at La Carta de Oaxaca include house-made tortillas with rice, chicken, or pork and the house-made mole sauce; the halibut tacos (particularly popular in the summer); and the

Serving food born from family tradition, La Carta de Oaxaca treats you like family with each dish that hits the table.

pork stew, posole, a pork stew that, Dominguez says, "feels all good when it's cold outside." Like a small home serving meals during the holidays, La Carta Carta de Oaxaca offers a sense of reprieve amidst the concrete construction occurring seemingly everywhere else in the city.

5431 Ballard Ave. NW
(206) 782-8722
lacartadeoaxaca.com

THE TEACHERS LOUNGE

Ironically, Desiree and Perryn Wright, founders of the Greenwood neighborhood's themed establishment The Teachers Lounge learned a thing or two opening their new spot. The married couple, who had worked for years as cocktail specialists, opened their school-themed spot in 2013, but the place took a few years to get off the ground, and the drink specialists had to take on the reins as kitchen managers too.

"We were working with a lot of interesting and unusual alcohol and liquors," Desiree says. "We found ourselves having to explain what was in the drinks, what the effects and origins were. We felt like we were teachers of booze, which is where the whole idea for the restaurant came from."

Desiree says she and her husband fell in love with the "sleepy" Greenwood neighborhood at the time because it reminded of them of Ballard before all the cranes and development came in, but the quiet Greenwood caused the lounge to struggle for a few years before finally taking off. "It's mellow," Desiree says, "more blue collar." The Wrights can relate. "We love analog and tactile stuff," she says. "We're old school that way."

Now the eatery is taking off. "It's been great," Desiree says. "At first, we weren't sure whether we were going to make it, but now we run everything. That really helped us feel more confident and have more control and to feel a sense of pride. Making not just the drinks but every piece of food that goes out, and with that came a little bit of cachet and respect from the neighborhood. They knew we wanted to make this work."

With the growth of the establishment comes the growth of the customer base. "Our regulars call themselves the Homeroom Homies," Desiree says, "which we love." Menu items that the Homies love, she adds, are the now infamous soup program. "I'm making a French onion today," Desiree notes. "Yesterday, it was Irish

With textbooks and a yellow school bus stop sign in the window, this homeroom-inspired restaurant will have you feeling nostalgic for sure.

potato. Before that it was sweet potato and corn. We have thirty recipes we rotate seasonally now."

Other favorite items include the house mac and cheese and grilled cheese—all simple, delicious dishes you'd want to eat, ironically, if you were home from school for the day. Nevertheless, it seems that the Teachers Lounge education is really paying off for everyone involved. "We have a really great clientele," Desiree affirms, "and the neighborhood is just growing. We took a chance on quiet Greenwood, and we're glad we did."

8505 Greenwood Ave. N
(206) 706-2880
teachersloungeseattle.com

OOINK

If you ask Chong Ooi, co-owner of Ooink Ramen in Capitol Hill, simplicity concerning food is comforting, affordable, and accessible, but that doesn't make it easy to create. "Simple needs time and craft," Ooi says, "and lots of patience."

Growing up, Ooi, who moved to the States in 2001 and worked as an Uber driver and meal deliverer before opening his über-popular noodle shop in the bustling Emerald City neighborhood in 2016, often ate noodles. "Like how Americans eat pizza here," says Ooi, who began professionally pursuing cooking in 2008, studying at Le Cordon Blue Hollywood before later taking an internship in Paris and then a fine dining job in New York City. Ever the humble chef, Ooi says, "When I began, I was nobody. I couldn't charge twenty to thirty dollars a plate. I had to make something simple. Comfort food."

The foundation for Ooi's cooking today, which he perfected in Hawaii before he came to Seattle, is hearty pork-based broths, and if you ask him, he'll quickly go into detail about skimming blood and other things off the top of boiling water, cleaning femur bones, creating the perfect six-and-a-half-minute egg, and the twenty-six hours it takes to make a proper stock. More than anything, though, even more than amazing dishes such as his kotteri ramen with Hawaiian sea salt and spicy mapo tofu ramen with ground pork and chili oil, Ooi cares about the people he serves and the craft of cooking. "Noodles are for people who are in a hurry and just want to eat food," he says.

He's been working his craft so well that Ooink has earned quite a bit of street cred since his modest but delicious eatery opened, but

> "Simple needs time and craft," Ooi says, "and lots of patience."

Ooink ramen is unlike any other in Seattle with it's dark, rich broth and thick, rich cut of pork chashu.

Ooi would never let that go to his head. "As a chef," he says, "I just do my job, and I do my job the best I can. The other day we sold out at seven o'clock, and I'm so sorry for that, but I try my best. Thank God so many people are supporting us, but I still have to continue to do what I do."

Aside from feeding the people, Ooi aims to keep the craft of cooking alive for the next generations. "I want to teach this craft for a younger generation," he says. "People think they can come from culinary school and become a chef. No, you cannot. You have to learn patience and dedication. You have to learn from your grandma. That's how I learned. It's only people like that who can teach you the craft."

1416 Harvard Ave.
(206) 568-7669
ooinkramen.com

CHEESE WIZARDS

William "Bo" Saxbe opened up his grilled cheese–focused food truck with his brother Tom in 2012. Before starting their new business, Bo had just lost his job as a scientist, and his brother had just moved to Seattle for love. "We were both footloose and fancy-free," says Bo. "So we decided to start our own business." Building up their food truck, however, took longer than they had anticipated. The two had to navigate many errors, such as buying equipment that required more energy than their generator could put out. Eventually, though, their hard work paid off, and they have one of the most popular trucks in the Emerald City.

"Before opening the truck," says Bo, "we wanted to make replica vintage field artillery pieces, but we decided that probably wouldn't be the most lucrative endeavor. Our mom actually suggested the food truck." The Saxbe brothers decided on their grilled cheese model because once the breads and cheeses and meats were sliced, there wouldn't be much labor in the truck itself. It's a simple concept, but simplicity requires the best ingredients to succeed. "We wanted something that would be really satisfying," says Bo, "but that wouldn't require a lot of kitchen time."

With a nerdy comic book–loving sensibility, the brothers created a menu that offers popular items such as The Goblin King with Swiss, Monterey Jack, cream cheese, roasted red peppers, chicken breast, and sriracha black pepper aioli; and The Voldemortadella with provolone and mozzarella, cream cheese, mortadella, salami, and Black Forest ham. Other side items include hot soup, such

> "Before opening the truck," says Bo, "we wanted to make replica vintage field artillery pieces, but we decided that probably wouldn't be the most lucrative endeavor."

Left: Take the mind and skill of an artist and apply it to one of the most beloved sandwiches and you have the delicious Cheese Wizards grilled cheese.

Right: Be on the look out for the giant yellow food truck filled with cheese!

as Tomato Basil Power-Up and bacon that's "our highest level of flavor magic."

Bo says he and his brother tried to approach the menu with streamlined precision, adding that "people crave simplicity, and a lot of restaurants don't really think about that." The aim of the truck is to showcase the bread, meats, and cheeses and to bring a quick and easy feeling of comfort to their patrons, many of whom regularly endure six months in the rainy Seattle weather.

While the duo have learned how to work in a kitchen, how to be mechanics, and how to advertise their small business, the biggest lesson they learned has to do with interacting with their loving customers. "The biggest secret to our success," says Bo, "is that we stay really engaged every day. We live in an age when most of our food is mass-produced, but we think human connection is really important, especially when it comes to food."

3204 Fifteenth Ave. W
(206) 949-4024
wizardsofcheese.com

SEÑOR MOOSE

In Seattle, new buildings and new businesses pop up all the time all around you. Many are new projects started by eager chefs or businesspeople looking for a new challenge. Other times, though, the businesses have all the pedigree anyone could want. When Camila Aguirre's mother, Kathleen Andersen, opened Señor Moose (then CaféMoose) in Seattle's Ballard neighborhood in 2004, right before the area's real estate boom, she had all the experience she needed and then some.

"My mother started it because that's what she knows how to do," says Aguirre, "and it was a once-in-a-lifetime opportunity. The building at the time was very cheap rent." Aguirre's mother and her mother's parents, she says, have been in the restaurant business since the sixties. After opening her restaurant, Andersen served American-style breakfasts for the first year, but having lived in Mexico for years with her husband, she was also an expert at making Mexican home cooking, which she began serving to her regulars on a lark. It took off. "They were like, 'What are you doing? You should be serving this instead!'" So she did.

In 2013, Aguirre took over Señor Moose so that her mother could move back to Mexico. Already with years of the industry and cooking to her name—"I grew up under the tables," she laughs—Aguirre has continued her mother's vision of the restaurant, which means putting the cooks first, continuing the tradition of serving street food and home cooking, and offering weekend brunch, a menu wrinkle not many south-of-the-border restaurants offer in the Emerald City. "I'm striving to keep it unique," Aguirre says, "for it not to become trendy, for it to remain somewhere where you can just be normal and still eat amazing food."

Señor Moose's brunch, which features some of the restaurant's best and most popular dishes, such as chilaquiles and corn with melty

166

The "Taquitos Dorados de Papa" dinner special is one of many palate pleasing dinner options you may find at this bona fide eatery.

cream, known as *esquites*, is important for Aguirre to keep going. "It's often the only time people who live outside the city can come visit us," she says. "People who would come to Ballard just to eat with us and bring their family."

Family supports and teaches each other, and this is what the Señor Moose pedigree is based on. "My mother is big and white with blue eyes," Aguirre says, "and she found herself in the middle of a tiny town in Mexico where there was nobody. All she could do was talk about food, and she was invited into people's kitchens."

5242 Leary Ave. NW
(206) 784-5568
senormoose.com

When he lived in Nashville, owner Jake Manny didn't have a car. As he began to build up a new bar, which he called Crying Wolf, Manny would walk to one of the three places nearby for lunch. One spot was the famous Bolton's, one of the two best Nashville hot chicken restaurants in the city. Manny was soon hooked.

Despite his love of Nashville and its famed hot chicken, Manny knew he needed to return to Seattle and the Northwest, where most of his family lived. "My family is from here," Manny says, "and everybody is getting older—nieces, nephews, Mom, and Dad—so I wanted a project to come back to."

So Manny brought his love of "addictive" Nashville hot chicken to the Emerald City. "I just think it's perfect," he says. Manny details a rigorous seasoning and cooking regimen when describing how hot chicken is made. While some aspects remain proprietary and secret, he uses words like "brining" and "dredge" and "chock full of flavor," and when it's finished, Manny says, "there are different levels of heat spices. That's really where the magic happens. Everything melds together." The flavor, he adds, is "more immediate" in how it hits the tongue.

While the food, from the fried chicken to the smoked Gouda mac and cheese, is supremely important to Manny, the foundation of his restaurant—that it maintains family sensibilities—is perhaps even more important. "Restaurants in general," he says, "are family affairs. It's a personal thing for me. I want everyone in tune with each other, caring about each other from the get-go. I want to treat everything with love."

That goes for the cocktails, too, one of which is a Carnivore Bloody Mary involving a big chicken wing poking out of the glass. Indeed, it's the chicken that makes Sisters and Brothers a destination, and that draw comes from Nashville. "In Nashville,"

Enjoy classic Nashville hot chicken at this West Seattle eatery. And add a side of greens so your mother's happy.

says Manny, "you can get hot chicken in a lot of places, but there are only a few heavy hitters. Bolton's, Prince's. It's Nashville's official dish," and Nashville, like Seattle, is bigger today than ever. "Before, most people who would go visit wouldn't go to the places where hot chicken was. Now the city is spread out, and it's more available." Thanks to Manny, the hot chicken dish has spread as far out as the Pacific Northwest too.

1128 S Albro Pl.
(206) 762-3767
sistersandbrothersbar.com

POMODORO RISTORANTE ITALIANO

Chef and owner Antolin Blanco is a night owl. This fact, perhaps more than any other, has informed how he manages his restaurant and comes up with new menu ideas. "I've hated every morning job I've ever had," says Blanco, "so I had to figure out a way to do business without getting up early."

Trained originally as a cook in the Spanish army, Blanco, after leaving the service, took jobs in Spain, England, and the United States. He's worked as a busser, server, sous chef, apprentice, and everything else under the restaurant sun, but when he decided to open Pomodoro, which offers a unique mixture of Spanish and Italian fare in Seattle's Eastlake neighborhood, the task of owning his own spot became very real and very difficult. "We used to sit by the window to let people know we weren't closed," he says, "and if someone came in, we'd get up and take care of them." Blanco struggled his first few years, but some smart advertising and a shift away from lunch to late-night dining helped him establish his eatery.

Wanting to open a Spanish-style-only restaurant, Blanco decided on a compromise of Spanish and popular Italian food. Sticking with the Mediterranean theme, he thought Italian would be more recognizable right off the bat. "I didn't have the money to be only Spanish," he said. "So we did tapas and pasta." Some of the menu ideas, Blanco says, come to him before bed as he's hunting around for a midnight snack. "If I go to bed hungry, I can't sleep," he says. "I'll be up all night in bed thinking and thinking. My brain is like a

> "We used to sit by the window to let people know we weren't closed," he says, "and if someone came in, we'd get up and take care of them."

Whether a heaping plate of penne with vodka sauce or whole mushrooms grilled in Spanish sherry, Pomodoro's fare always contains quintessential Mediterranean flavors.

turbo engine. That's when I come up with the best and most popular recipes."

While the Eastlake neighborhood has risen and grown up all around Pomodoro, which opened up in 1995, the foundation of Blanco's recipes has largely remained consistent. Yet he often adds new specials, such as a hummus and truffle-filled giant ravioli or a halibut ceviche. "It's a mix of South American, Asian, European, and American," he says. "All kinds of flavors that contrast with each other. Every time we serve it people go 'Wow, wow, wow!'"

For Blanco, being distinct is supremely important. He appreciates experimentation and uniqueness over the standard. His carbonara, for example, doesn't involve the traditional egg yolk ingredient. "If you come to our restaurant and have a certain dish and you want to have it again, you have to come back to Pomodoro," he says. "You can't get it at any other place. My food has my own distinctiveness, and that's what I like about it."

2366 Eastlake Ave. E
(206) 324-3160
pomodoro.net

13 COINS

In the fifty-plus years that 13 Coins, one of the city's only twenty-four-hour restaurants, has resided in the South Lake Union neighborhood, it's seen it all. Famous celebrities, from professional athletes to writers to movie stars, have all slid into the tall booths and enjoyed a late-night meal, and when Albert Moscatel (and partners) purchased the historic restaurant in 2005, all he wanted was to continue that legacy. Now, just this year, Moscatel moved the restaurant to Pioneer Square near the historic King Street Station in the hopes that it will last there at least another fifty years.

Moscatel remembers two distinct eras in his life when 13 Coins was important. His family worked in the furniture business for more than sixty years near the restaurant, and during that time, he'd often go to 13 Coins with his father for lunch. Also, when he got older, he would go to the all-night eatery late for meals while working overtime. "I'd get Joe's Special, chicken Parmesan and French onion soup," he recalls.

13 Coins, he says, is both a twenty-four-hour meeting place and a family restaurant with "a lot of happy memories." It's also a place where patrons can watch live music and eat a meal or hide in a tall booth under the dim lights and scarf a meal before or after an event. "We try to offer something for anybody at any time they want to come in," explains Moscatel, before noting that there are more than a hundred items on the 13 Coins menu. "If you want French toast at one in the morning, you can get it. It's what you want when you want."

Some of those one-hundred-plus items making up the menu that offers "something for everybody" include pork belly sliders, chicken ribs, fried artichoke hearts, a one-pound bucket of Manila clams with pesto, coconut prawns, buttermilk fried chicken, beef

Whether you're arriving famished for a big meal or meeting for drinks and deep conversation, the twenty-four-hour hot spot 13 Coins has it all.

stroganoff, jambalaya, eggs Benedict, and about ninety-seven other things. As the new Pioneer Square location continues to settle into its foundation, Moscatel says it's important for the historic restaurant to continue to grow and change with the times. "I think it's really important right now that we are contemplating and enhancing our menu," he says. "We want to offer some wonderful new items while also keeping the oldies but goodies. We have to keep evolving. If we do that, I think we'll be around here another fifty years."

255 S King St.
(206) 682-2513
13coins.com

ANCHOR END PRETZEL SHOPPE

Twin sisters Amanda and Jessica Lewis were tired of working hard and not getting the respect they deserved, so they did something about it. "I was a kitchen manager for a long time in Ballard," says Amanda, "and Jessica worked at a bunch of bakeries in the city. We were just always the most hardworking at our jobs and always kind of got crapped on, for lack of a better term. So we said we wanted to work for ourselves. We knew we could, and we did."

The two sisters opened up their truck in 2015, based on an idea Amanda had when she was nineteen and living in Upstate New York. "There was this abandoned movie theater," she says, "that I dreamed about taking over even though it was condemned. I wanted to open it up, play B-movies, and serve twists on movie theater food. One of those twists was a pretzel bun sandwich."

Amanda and Jessica later moved to Seattle to be closer to family. When the idea for the truck came up, they jumped at the idea and decided to go with the pretzel bun sandwich theme—to the benefit of the business. Because they are both boiled and baked, pretzels make for sturdier buns than most sandwich bread. "There's a nice chewy texture," Amanda says, "but it also holds up way better, which allows us to go really big."

The most popular item on the truck, Amanda says, is their play on a Cuban sandwich, which includes pulled pork, pork belly, pickled jalapeños, dill pickles, stone-ground mustard, and Swiss cheese, but the coup de grâce is that the sandwich is served on a cinnamon and

> "We try with all our sandwiches," Amanda says, "to hit as many tastes as we can."

174

At Anchor End, you can get all of your favorite sandwich ingredients put together on one-of-a-kind pretzel bread. Whaaattt??!!!

sugar pretzel bun to tie it together. "We try with all our sandwiches," Amanda says, "to hit as many tastes as we can." Other delicious menu items include the Seasquab, with a fried egg, Monterey jack cheese, and maple aioli, and the Resistor, with slow-braised cold-cut brisket with tomato jam, arugula, and pickled onions.

While having the kitschy eye-catching detail of pretzel bun sandwiches does draw customers to the food truck, Amanda says it's through her and her sister's hard work that success has come their way. "I think the best way for you to stand out is just working your butt off," she says, "and that's what we do. If you're a woman, you often have to work three times as hard to get noticed and taken seriously. That's what pushes us."

anchorendseattle.com

WALLYBURGER

Owner Gary Reynolds cares about two things: simplicity and vibe. Reynolds owns and operates Seattle's Electrokitty studio, where artists like Dave Matthews and Nas have recorded music, but he also runs two eateries in the Emerald City: his Revolver bar, which focuses on drinks and vinyl records, and Wallyburger, a tried-and-true burger joint in the city's Wallingford neighborhood.

While the restaurant offers a hearty selection of burgers whose toppings range from lettuce and tomato to fried jalapeños and queso sauce, Reynolds believes with burgers, no matter the heft of the ingredients, there should be balance, simplicity, and clarity. "I'm a firm believer in picking a couple ingredients that complement each other," says Reynolds. "It's like mixing music. If you have a few instruments, they can all shine. If you have a ton of players, everything has to get small, and they interfere with each other."

Wallyburger, which opened in the summer of 2017, offers classic American fare, all the way down to the chili cheese fries, but the atmosphere of the place, which is small and includes a few tables and booths, is friendly with a touch of the Old West, which makes sense since Reynolds grew up in Texas. He says Wallyburger uses a spice mix from Texas in all their burgers. "It adds this nice smoky flavor to it," he says. "I believe it's the best seasoning a burger can get. I grew up with it."

Offering a particular type of experience is the fundamental key to success when owning a bar or restaurant, Reynolds explains. "When people go out to eat, for instance," he says, "they want to go somewhere else, whether it's walking into a burger joint or going into

> I'm a firm believer in picking a couple ingredients that complement each other," says Reynolds. "It's like mixing music. If you have a few instruments, they can all shine."

Get a big, satisfying, and hearty burger at this Western-themed Wallingford hole-in-the-wall. Photo credit: Morgen Schuler

a five-star restaurant. You're paying for the experience." Specificity, in this way, is paramount. "You want a burger: think Wallyburger," Reynolds says. "Just like if you want a beer and a classic rock record: you go to Revolver."

While this philosophy of distinction is likely correct, Reynolds, who, before ever opening an eatery, used to cook his "Gary's Gumbo" for the popular live music spot the Seamonster Lounge, knows it's not just about perception or advertising. "When you open up a new place," he says, "you experience a huge bump. Everyone comes in and tries it. Then you get some people that stick and frequent your restaurant. After that, you're in the process of building up repeat customers. I'm really big on atmosphere. All my businesses have to have a great feel."

1719 N Forty-Fifth St.
(206) 588-0696
wallyburgerseattle.com

HOTEL ALBATROSS

amous for its puffy taco window, Hotel Albatross is the perfect confluence of all things Ballard past, present, and future. The neighborhood, once known as just a sleepy little fishing community, is now experiencing a great deal of development both upward and outward. Facing this reality, Ballard business owner Drew Church got together with two other local business owners and bought the building that would later become the popular tiki bar. "We wanted to control what was going to go into that vacant building," says Church. So, Hotel Albatross was born.

The restaurant and bar, which feature regular live music and comedy, offer their signature puffy tacos filled with veggies (and refried beans, chipotle crema, and cotija cheese), steak, or chorizo. They are sold inside in the traditional sit-down area or from the window outside for street traffic. "The puffy taco is part of our whole menu concept," says Church, a twenty-year Ballard bartending veteran, "which is based on the world's drinking and street food. There's some Asian options, Latin, and Mexican influences. We didn't want to be pinned down." To go along with their myriad street food options, the bar also offers cocktails served as you'd expect and want them: in a coconut with a giant straw and mini umbrella.

Other than the popular puffy tacos, other delicious (though potentially sloppy) menu items include the totchos—or, a plate of nachos, but instead of tortilla chips, it's made with tater tots—as well as tonkotsu ramen with pork belly, soy egg, and fried onions. If these items seem odd for a bar in the middle of Ballard, Church might agree with you. "As much as I am a Luddite," he says, "I know we kind of have to roll with the punches and evolve."

So, for the restaurant that could have been an eyesore, say, another Starbucks or even a Friday's, amidst the already existing businesses owned by Church and his two Albatross co-owners, the tiki bar

Whether you're feasting on their signature totchos (tater tot nachos) or their puffy tacos, Hotel Albatross is the perfect late night dining spot.

and restaurant maintain a sense of weird Ballard while also offering something new (and puffy!). "Change is inevitable," offers Church. "Of course, there's been a lot of positive change in the neighborhood. It would obviously be bad to just complain about that change. It's way better to try and steer things in a direction that we think is cool."

2319 NW Market St.
(206) 566-6181
hotelalbatross.com

OFF THE REZ

The city of Seattle is named after Chief Seattle, or Seathl, head of the Duwamish and Suquamish tribes in the mid-nineteenth century. The Pacific Northwest has a long (and sordid) history with native people. As the country continues to grow and examine its historical treatment of indigenous people, there are ways to honor and celebrate Native Americans. One of those ways is through food, and that's where the food truck Off the Rez comes into play.

Started in 2012, the popular food truck, owned and operated by Cecilia Rikard and her longtime boyfriend, Mark McConnell, whose mother grew up on the Blackfeet Reservation in Montana, focuses on fry bread and Indian tacos as well as a rotating menu of specials. "Mark and I are naturally entrepreneurial," Rikard says, "and we both really love food. Back then at that time, the Seattle food truck scene had just gotten moving. It wasn't anything like it is today."

Rikard says McConnell grew up loving fry bread and Indian tacos. "We like to say," says Rikard, "everyone says their auntie or grandma has the best fry bread recipe." Their own recipe consists of a flour shell, fried to make it puffy, which is then topped with veggies, sour cream, and other fixings. "Mark craved the Indian tacos he knew from a kid, but nobody in Seattle was offering them anywhere. So we thought, 'Oh, this is a natural idea. Let's do this!'"

Upon opening the truck, she says, the duo fielded question after question about their fare. "When we opened, we didn't realize how many people were unfamiliar with fry bread and Indian tacos," Rikard says, but this curiosity turned into fascination, which turned into a good buzz for the business that hopes to continue growing. The couple may even open a brick-and-mortar location in the future while maintaining their high-volume catering operations.

Along with the bread and tacos, Off the Rez offers regular specials based on traditional native dishes, which can involve

Authentic Native American-inspired fare eaten in the heart of the Pacific Northwest is the perfect way to celebrate modern-day Seattle. Photo credit: Morgen Schuler

huckleberries, wild rice, buffalo, and "dry meat," or jerky. Its menu has caused the city to take notice and led the group to win an Innovation Award from local publication the *Seattle Weekly*. "At first, we didn't know what to expect," says Rikard, "but on our first day when we opened our service windows, we quickly had a line of ten to fifteen people. That was when we first looked at each other and said, 'Hey, this could really work out! There's people here who actually want to eat our food.'"

8509 Roosevelt Way NE
offthereztruck.com

THE WHALE WINS

The charming corner restaurant in the stroller-friendly Fremont neighborhood is often a sight to behold. With big, bright windows that let the light in (when there is natural light in Seattle!), Renee Erickson's the Whale Wins is one of a handful of restaurants that the James Beard Award winner owns and operates. While the eatery stands on its own, its wholesome feel and charming aesthetic is connected to all of Erickson's projects.

The chef opened the Whale Wins, which focuses on wood-fired ovens and vegetable-friendly fare, on Halloween in 2012. While no one dressed up for the opening, Erickson laughs, "We were just happy to be open." Erickson, who grew up in the Pacific Northwest, says she'd wanted to cook with a wood-fire oven after spending years working with seafood (and opening her popular oyster restaurant, the Walrus and the Carpenter in 2010). "I fell in love with some restaurants in London," she says, "that focused on a lot of vegetables and the combination of vegetables in wood ovens, specifically trying to create foods with a complex flavor without them being too heavy."

The wood-fired oven gave Erickson "new parameters" to cook within, offering a challenge. "I was really intrigued," she says, "with cooking out of my comfort zone. The wood oven is pretty magical, something people underestimate. It's usually thought of just for pizza, but we've never made a pizza in it. The oven gives a richness and a softness to the food we prepare, whereas grilling over wood can be a lot harder on the food."

Erickson said she learned the ins and outs of the wood oven at the popular and upscale Ballard pizzeria Delancey on the eatery's off days, "but we put our fire in the back," she says, "whereas most pizza places bank it on the side to get the heat to convect in a different way."

Erickson says she grew a fondness for vegetables, and those items like oysters that you can just pluck from the earth as a child, learning about food and how to grow it. At the restaurant, popular menu

Chef Renee Erickson, the visionary behind the elevated, rustic cuisine at the Whale Wins. Photo credit: Morgen Schuler

items include sardine toast made with roasted tomato curry with a fennel salad; a salt-crusted, oven-roasted chicken; and zucchini bread, which is offered as a dessert and excites the palate with a buttery, crispy, smoky edge and is served with crème fraiche and sea salt. "I spent a lot of time around the water growing up," Erickson says, "eating really simple foods, and when I cook for people, I'm not overly intrigued by gadgets. I'm trying to make the freshest food and present it in the nicest and most beautiful ways I can. That's more important than any trick."

3506 Stone Way N
(206) 632-9425
thewhalewins.com

LUC

When you've been in the restaurant industry in a city for over three decades, as Thierry Rautureau (aka the Chef in the Hat) has, you learn a few things, and then you learn a few more things. Rautureau, a James Beard Award winner who has been featured on the famed television show *Top Chef*, moved to Seattle from France some thirty years ago. Since then, he's owned and operated three favorite local restaurants (two of which remain open today) and served hundreds of thousands of plates.

Rautureau's restaurant Luc, located in the swanky Madison Valley neighborhood, opened in 2010. It's a lovely corner restaurant that the chef hoped would resemble the neighborhood spots he cherished as a young man in France. "My idea for Luc was to be a friendly, affordable, comfortable bistro," he says. "To build a place where people would gather and come without any pretention. If you live within a mile and you're hungry or thirsty, it's a no-brainer. Just walk right in."

Luc's menu offers favorites of all kinds, from the classic boeuf Bourguignon stew to crepes to one of their claims to fame, a basket of soufflé potato crisps, or delicious puffed-up steak fries. "I used to make those in 1980 when I was in Chicago," Rautureau says. "It was my job every Monday. I made pan after pan of this beautiful stuff. I got really good at it, though they can be pretty temperamental."

Like every other area in the city, Madison Valley is growing and changing, causing Rautureau to think about new ways each day to keep Luc flourishing. "When I started here thirty years ago," he says,

> "My idea for Luc was to be a friendly, affordable, comfortable bistro. To build a place where people would gather and come without any pretention." – Thierry Rautureau

Luc is famous for its soufflé potatoes, a puffed-up, gourmet version of French fries.
Photo credit: Morgen Schuler

"everything was mostly just some houses. Now every house has a duplex and triplex on it." While this means more customers in the immediate neighborhood, it also signals a morphing Seattle that restaurateurs all over the city have to contemplate.

Nevertheless, Luc remains a jewel in its cozy neighborhood. "We have to remain consistent in our service," Rautureau notes. "Hospitality and comfort are very important, especially at Luc. I always say that it often takes people ten minutes to walk from the front door to the back of the restaurant because people see so many friends they know," and this all comes from the top down. "I'm a guy who loves to make people happy," Rautureau says. "If I was meant to be a millionaire, it wasn't in this life. This life I'm working my butt off!"

2800 E Madison St.
(206) 328-6645
thechefinthehat.com/luc/

SUSHI KAPPO TAMURA

If it weren't for his mother sleeping in on Sunday mornings, sushi chef Taichi Kitamura might not have ever found his calling. The co-owner of Eastlake's Sushi Kappo Tamura, which opened in 2010, Kitamura began cooking eggs for his family when he was in third grade. "The rest of my family was already up, and I was hungry," Kitamura recalls, "so I just started cooking breakfast for the family."

From then on, he says, he took every chance he could to cook. "I didn't think I was going to be a chef," he says. "I just loved it." Kitamura later found himself a student at Seattle University and working for famed local chef Shiro Kashiba, one of the most well-respected sushi chefs in the world. "I thought," says Kitamura, "I wanted to be happy like he is."

Sushi Kappo Tamura, which is based out of an open kitchen, rotates its fare seasonally and features locally sourced vegetables, including herbs from its rooftop garden, and fish, such as salmon or halibut. "*Kappo* means open kitchen," Kitamura says. "It's the only way to enjoy it. The sushi chef makes sushi and serves it directly to the customers. The same goes for hot food. If you try good tempura, the only way to eat it is over the counter when it's really hot. With an open kitchen, you can do that."

Further, the open kitchen, Kitamura notes, also offers the opportunity for him and his staff to get to know the customers better, more closely, which then allows them to customize the menu properly to their tastes. "I built the restaurant so we'd be able to do that," the chef says. To create the perfect sushi, the chef explains, "it all comes down to quality ingredients and bringing out the best flavor from good ingredients without masking the original flavor. That's the core philosophy of sushi or Japanese cooking in general."

To teach this to new chefs, Kitamura says he likes to impart a simple ethic, similar to that of famed fashion designer Coco

This sushi house's menu is clean and crisp and its owner is as friendly a master chef as any in the Emerald City. Photo credit: Morgen Schuler

Chanel, who said, "Before you leave the house, look in the mirror and take one thing off." Echoing this idea, foodwise, Kitamura explains, "When you end up cooking with the best products, keep it simple. When you start cooking, you want to add all sorts of ingredients, but as I learned to do it, I just stayed with the basics. That's what makes my restaurant unique."

2968 Eastlake Ave. E
(206) 547-0937
sushikappotamura.com

JEMIL'S BIG EASY

For chef Jemil Johnson, variety truly is the spice of life. "One thing about being a chef," the food truck owner says, "is that you have to be able to taste cultures from all over." Speaking with Johnson, one gets the sense that this isn't so much an obligation as it is a joy for him.

Johnson, who grew up in New Orleans, left his hometown at eighteen to join the military. "I got to travel," he says, and after growing up sampling dishes in his mother's kitchen or his auntie's restaurant, Johnson got to taste cuisines from all over during his service. Eventually, he landed back in the Big Easy and began working in hotels and restaurants all over the city. When a friend said there was a gig in Seattle at a new eatery, Johnson jumped at the chance. "I always knew I'd end up in Seattle," he says. "I saw it on a map one day, and I just knew."

Ensconced in the Emerald City, Johnson later took a trip to Portland, Oregon, and found himself touring the local food truck scene. The experience, he said, showed him that food trucks can be more family and community oriented with a more nimble menu. "I'm not a trendy person," he says, "but this was something special." In Portland, Johnson tried "everything that had any Cajun lineage," he says. "That's my forte," but he knew there was room for him in the PNW.

Since opening his truck in Seattle, Johnson says he's traveled all over, from Oregon to Washington and from the east side to the west side of the state sharing his recipes born out of his travels as a young man. Popular items on his regular menu include crawfish étouffée, blackened catfish, and blackened chicken, he says. But more than that, regulars to the truck often enjoy the rotating specials, he says. "We might do a Cajun shepherd's pie one day," he explains, "or a stuffed pork loin on another. Or a bayou burger stuffed with shrimp."

Step up to the bright and happy yellow truck for some of Jemil's bayou-inspired cuisine.
Photo credit: Morgen Schuler

As the years pass by, though, the food truck is only growing, and while it's on the road often, Johnson is asked more and more to cater. "Food truck weddings," he says, "they're more and more popular. It's one of the reasons we're so successful, and with us, there's variety to every plate. We can do everything, from chateaubriand to popcorn crawfish. We have a vast repertoire, and we like to accommodate."

(206) 641-6551
jemilsbigeasy.com

MODERNIST CUISINE

Right from the start, let's make sure this is clear: Modernist Cuisine isn't a regular restaurant open to the public. In fact, it's not a restaurant at all. Instead, it's a research laboratory and publishing house founded by former Microsoft executive Nathan Myhrvold. His goal was to amass a team and create the "missing text" of modern cooking techniques—almost like how Julia Child created the first English version of French cooking. While customers can't order off any menu at the Bellevue Willy Wonka-esque facility, it is more than worth a chapter in this humble tome due to both its proximity to Seattle and its impact on the culinary world.

"*Modernist Cuisine: The Art and Science of Cooking* broke many of the rules for cookbooks," Myhrvold explains of the text that took three years to produce and clocks in at nearly 2,500 pages. "Within the first year of release, we had to return to press three times for additional printings. It won numerous major food-writing awards and has been translated into nine languages." Since the first book, Myhrvold, who is also famous for going on paleontology expeditions and digging up dinosaur bones, has published follow-up epics, including *Modernist Cuisine at Home, The Photography of Modernist Cuisine,* and *Modernist Bread,* all of which "helped make the concepts behind avant-garde cooking and food science even more widely available," he says. *Modernist Pizza* is said to be next on the way.

Led by head chef Francisco Migoya and Myhrvold, the team has focused on experimental cooking ideas and questions. "They still prepare highly challenging thirty-course dinners every once in a while," says Myhrvold of his chefs, "but most of their work focuses on developing new recipes, exploring new techniques, and making these ideas accessible to chefs and food lovers." The images of these creations, like a blender cut in half lengthwise filled with Roma tomatoes, are stunning, and certain findings by the kitchen, such as what liquid nitrogen can do to popcorn, are eye-popping.

The Modernist Cuisine Kitchen is where many of the mind-bending food experiments take place with chef–author Nathan Myhrvold.

The key to the experimental process, says Myhrvold, who has been featured on such popular cooking programs as *Top Chef*, is using scientific doubt to get to the root of why certain food combinations and cooking techniques work and others do not. "We have found that the most effective way to make rapid progress in cooking is to understand how the relevant science of its processes works," Myhrvold offers. "We have also been fortunate enough to draw on the expertise of a wide range of talented chemists, biologists, physicists, computational analysts, machinists, and others at the Intellectual Ventures Laboratory as well as in academia and industry."

What is the most interesting thing he's learned through the process? "Taking a skeptical, curious attitude toward food is actually really helpful," he says. "By critically examining long-standing culinary lore, we not only learned facts but also came across a lot of myths guiding the way people cook, bake, and think about food." Is there an example? Of course! "Have you ever heard that the water in New York City is the secret to good bagels?" Myhrvold continues. "We put that notion to the scientific test and found that the type of water you use doesn't matter." Finally, he says, "These explorations have opened the door to many discoveries, and some have led to new techniques that are revolutionary."

14360 SE Eastgate Way, Bellevue
modernistcuisine.com/about-modernist-cuisine/

THE CRUMPET SHOP

"It's funny that we're in the crumpet business," says Robin Lasater, manager of Pike Place Market's longtime eatery. Lasater, whose family opened the shop in 1976, says that despite the funny name and the niche product, crumpets were the dream business for his parents long ago. "My father was playing around with ideas of what business to open," he says. "Then my parents took a honeymoon to England. When they came back, my dad bought a recipe, and the rest is history."

In the forty-two years the Crumpet Shop has stood in downtown Seattle, little has changed. The kitchen has gotten a little smaller, and a few more seats have been added, and the business started using organic flour a handful of years ago, but besides that, it's remained classic through and through. "A crumpet is a traditional English griddle cake," explains Lasater, "with big circular holes in it. If you toast and butter it, the butter soaks in the holes, making it crispy and spongy, perfect for a topping. My parents always used to say when I was going up, 'It's not an English muffin. It's not a pancake. It's a crumpet!'"

Classic crumpets flying out of the store most mornings are topped with seasonal jams, preserves, and marmalade, "but the most popular," says Lasater, "is the homemade lemon curd and ricotta crumpet. Also the maple butter and cream cheese crumpet is real popular." There is even a breakfast green eggs and ham crumpet served with pesto. The plates are small, and the place is often packed, making for some rather close interactions in a city known to often avoid them. "My father wanted to own a small

> "My parents always used to say when I was going up 'It's not an English muffin. It's not a pancake. It's a crumpet!'"
> – Robin Lasater

They're not English muffins, they're not biscuits, they're … crumpets. And you can belly up to the counter at Pike Place Market for your fill. Photo credit: Morgen Schuler

place that would force people to mingle," Lasater laughs, "and so our shop is pretty small. When things get hustling and bustling, it can get pretty close."

While you're eating, you can witness the creation of dozens of crumpets. "There's a big window to our kitchen back here," Lasater says. "You can watch the crumpets get made anytime from 7:00 a.m. to about noon!" It becomes a popular show during breakfast hours as the Crumpet Shop's patrons squeeze into the tight quarters and order their first meal of the day. "I started helping out here in the mid-eighties," Lasater says. "I worked here through high school, and besides a short fishing career in Alaska, this has been my home."

1503 First Ave.
(206) 682-1598
thecrumpetshop.com

TRIPLE XXX
ROOTBEER DRIVE-IN

The Issaquah, Washington, business was failing until José Enciso stepped in one fateful day in 1999. "I was at a used equipment store, and I ran into this couple," he recalls. "The lady was a Latina, and we made eye contact and started talking. Latinos, we bond within minutes. They told me they had a restaurant, and they were trying to sell it, and they asked if I knew anybody."

So the two parties exchanged numbers, but a year went by, says Enciso, who had grown up a migrant cotton picker until he was about thirty years old (his family later owned restaurants in Oregon and Washington), "and I ran out of excuses why I didn't come over and look at it." Finally, though, he went to check it out without telling the owners. "I got a root beer, and I sat down, drank it slowly," he says. "I visualized the inside, what changes would be nice." Enciso finally agreed to buy the place, taking out a bank loan and putting his money where his mouth was.

Turns out, though, XXX Rootbeer is historic. The concept, which originally began in the thirties, was to have the unique beverage pair with the drive-in business model. Since then, the number of XXX Rootbeer locations has dwindled from seventy-nine to one—Enciso's—but before all that could transpire, he had to talk to his wife. So he brought her to XXX. "I told her," he says, "I have to share something with you. She said, 'Okay, what have you done now!'" At the time, Enciso had been a classic car collector ("Women don't understand men buying classic cars," he jokes), but he told her that "we own the place," and after a few months of dealing with the "silent treatment," Enciso and wife have happily operated XXX Rootbeer for nineteen years. "Telling my wife about

Everything in this throwback restaurant makes you say WOW—from the giant burgers to the perfectly made milkshakes.

the purchase," he recalls, "was the most grueling, slow-motion speechless, silent drive of my life!"

The restaurant has become one of the most beloved in the Seattle area, serving giant and messy hamburgers, huge milkshakes, and both French fries and onion rings. When you walk into the eatery, which hosts more than thirty-seven classic car shows a year, you see the thousands of stickers, toy cars hanging from the ceiling, and everything else kitschy that would make a guy or gal from the 1950s smile ear-to-ear. "Ninety-nine percent of the memorabilia hanging in the restaurant belongs to customers," Enciso says.

The secret to XXX Rootbeer's success, Enciso adds, is the *Wow* factor behind everything that the eye can see, from food to decorations to the overall vibe and energy. "Everything, the minute you walk in, has a *wow* behind it," he says. "You look through the door, you go, 'Wow!' You get a burger, you go, 'Wow!' It's been a really rewarding venture," Enciso notes, "and it's made a difference in many people's lives."

98 NE Gilman Blvd., Issaquah
(425) 392-1266
triplexrootbeer.com

HEAVEN SENT FRIED CHICKEN

Heaven Sent Fried Chicken, which opened in 2012, is operated by Ezell Stephens. If the name sounds familiar, it's because Stephens once owned and operated Ezell's Famous Fried Chicken, but after a split from his business partners, Stephens has moved on. In the time that passed, the quality and flavor at Ezell's has diminished somewhat, while Heaven Sent remains maybe the best place in the Seattle area to get the stuff. In other words, Ezell Stephens is the King of Fried Chicken in Seattle no matter where he's working.

When you ask Stephens why he called his restaurant Heaven Sent, he'll say, simply, "Because that's what it is!" Before any of that, though, before he opened his new restaurant (which has three locations around Seattle) and even before Ezell's opened, Stephens was a Texas native. After dropping out of high school, Stephens got a job frying chicken in a local restaurant, where he stayed for three years before joining the Coast Guard, an experience he credits for bringing him from the countryside to big ol' world. "But once I got out," he says, "the only thing I could remember that I loved doing was making fried chicken."

So, he moved to Seattle, where he had some friends, and opened his first restaurant. Then the unimaginable happened: world-famous Oprah Winfrey visited Ezell's. "She really liked it," Stephens says with a grin, "so she flew me out to Chicago to make it for her birthday. That was unbelievable. That's the kind of stuff you hear about, but you don't expect it to be you." Winfrey talked

> When you ask Stephens why he called his restaurant Heaven Sent, he'll say, simply, "Because that's what it is!"

Made by the Seattle fried chicken master himself, Ezell Stephens. Heaven Sent fried chicken truly is.

about Stephens on her show. "After that," he recalls, "the place went crazy. People were calling from everywhere. I've been playing catch-up ever since."

Without giving away the recipe, what does Stephens think is the secret to his famous fried chicken? "First," he says, "it starts with top-quality product, and everything you add to it has to be the same, from the oil to the spices, and then you finish it off with love. You have to love what you're doing," and the love doesn't just stop with Stephens. The Emerald City loves his food. The hottest items include his chicken strips (try the spicy ones) and creamy mac and cheese. "I was inspired by the Almighty himself," says Stephens. "That's where the name came from. It was given to me. I'm just carrying out the orders."

509 S Third St., Renton
(425) 917-3000
heavensentfriedchicken.com

OLIVER'S TWIST

While the Greenwood neighborhood eatery and cocktail bar has been open since 2007, it was only recently that Karuna Long took it over from the original proprietors. Long, an employee at Oliver's Twist for years, purchased the spot when the founders decided they wanted to sell. "It was serendipitous," says Long. "For me, I always wanted to open my own bar. I've always loved the story behind Oliver's Twist—how we do classic cocktails with our own flair and serve great food."

Born out of an English-centric, Charles Dickens theme, Oliver's Twist represents something of a dichotomy. On the one hand, the place is refined, elevated, classic in an everything-seems-very-valuable-in-here sort of feel, but in another way, the watering hole is very much smack-dab in the center of a residential Greenwood neighborhood with young parents pushing strollers and the burgeoning neighborhood growing and growing around it. As a result, the eatery has to walk a fine line, which it does quite well.

Long says he hopes his efforts sustaining and bolstering the bar will continue the legacy of the prior owners. "Oliver's Twist," he says, "is not just a neighborhood haunt. It's a place where I hope people, whether it's their hundredth time or first time, come in and get transported. I want the place to take them into a different area. Maybe they feel like they're not even in the U.S. anymore."

The community of people who have called Oliver's Twist their hangout home for years remains paramount for Long. "We get a lot of folks that come in and celebrate anniversaries, weddings," he says. "That kind of community is really exactly why I got into this industry and love it so much." When those people do walk through the bar's front door, they are expecting not just great interactions with people but also elegant cocktails and matching edible fare. "We have a play on a manhattan," Long says, "with rye whiskey,

This friendly neighborhood cocktail bar and eatery in North Seattle serves refined plates and expertly crafted drinks. Photo credit: Morgen Schuler

Averna, maraschino cherry liqueur, black pepper tincture, and orange bitters. It's delicious."

As for the food, the eatery is known far and wide for at least two of its sharable plates: the blue cheese and bacon-stuffed dates and the grilled cheese with a tomato soup cappuccino accompaniment. "We try," says Long, "to cultivate items that are fun, sharable plates that go with our traditional cocktails." In the end, however, for Long it always comes down to the nitty-gritty details of people sharing their lives with each other. "That's probably the best highlight," he says. "People really appreciate when you remember the small, minute details of their lives. Things you've shared in conversation. That's really the best."

6822 Greenwood Ave. N
(206) 706-6673
oliverstwistseattle.com

TOP POT DOUGHNUTS

When Mark Klebeck and his brother, Michael, opened the first Top Pot Doughnuts on Summit Avenue in Seattle's Capitol Hill neighborhood, they had no idea that their idea would blossom into nearly two dozen more locations, including one in Dallas, Texas, in about fifteen years. "Our growth," says Klebeck, "has been thoughtful. It's worked out really well. Other companies can be more aggressive, but I could never have seen doing this in just one or two years."

Mark and Michael, who both had experience running successful area coffee shops and who both grew up loving doughnuts, took the methodical approach to Top Pot. Opening a store or two each year, taking advantage of opportunities when they arose, but no store, no matter how it's run, can accrue the sort of breadth Top Pot has without having a good product. "In 2002," Klebeck says, "we didn't feel like there was any one company that was truly putting out great doughnuts in Seattle. There weren't really a lot around the country either." (SHOTS FIRED, DUNKIN DONUTS!!)

So they went to work and created Top Pot's top-notch doughnuts. With flavors ranging from the tried and true, such as maple bars and apple fritters, to the more odd and experimental, for example, seasonal pumpkin old-fashioneds and Ovaltine cream-filled, Klebeck says it's all about listening to his staff and customers. "The flavors are influenced by suggestions," he says, "from customers or employees. If we love them, especially as a staff, they'll likely succeed."

Klebeck likens the business in some ways to that of a microbrewery—something Seattle residents are quite accustomed to. "I love beer," Klebeck grins. "If you look at Seattle's Fremont

"The flavors are influenced by suggestions from customers or employees." – Mark and Michael Klebeck

Maybe nothing is more mouthwatering than an up-close shot of chocolate and glazed doughnuts. Photo credit: Morgen Schuler

Brewery, they may have different styles they put out that different customers gravitate toward. Like our bacon maple bars, some people think it's the most disgusting thing, but then another audience just loves it!"

Being in the doughnut game for nearly two decades means that some of Klebeck's customers, once children themselves, have grown up and are bringing their own children into the shops. "We have this employee orientation meeting once a month," he muses, "and we have employees that are fresh out of high school or in college working for us now, and they were coming in with their parents when they were two or three years old. It's pretty weird, but it's also really cool, even if it makes me feel a little old."

609 Summit Ave. E
(206) 323-7841
toppotdoughnuts.com

APPENDIX

UNIVERSITY DISTRICT:
Morsel, 24
XI'AN Noodles, 42

WALLINGFORD:
Pam's Kitchen, 22
Molly Moon's Ice Cream, 30
Dick's Drive-In, 52
Yoroshiku, 114
Wallyburger, 176

WEDGWOOD:
The Wedgwood Broiler, 80

WEST SEATTLE:
Roxbury Lanes, 8
Bok a Bok, 12
Marination, 46
Bakery Nouveau, 58
Easy Street Records Cafe, 78
Zippy's Giant Burgers, 118
Proletariat Pizza, 136
Sisters and Brothers, 168

RESTAURANTS IN ALPHABETICAL ORDER
WITH ADDRESSES

13 Coins:
255 S King St., Seattle, WA 98104

Alibi Room, The:
85 Pike St., Seattle, WA 98101

Anchor End Pretzel Shoppe:
Roaming food truck

Angry Beaver, The:
8412 Greenwood Ave. N, Seattle, WA 98103

Bakery Nouveau:
4737 California Ave. SW, Seattle, WA 98116

Bananas Grill:
4556 Martin Luther King Jr. Way S, Seattle, WA 98108

Beecher's Handmade Cheese:
1600 Pike Pl., Seattle, WA 98101

Beth's Cafe:
7311 Aurora Ave. N, Seattle, WA 98103

Bok a Bok:
1521 SW Ninety-Eighth St., Seattle, WA 98106

Capitol Cider:
818 E Pike St., Seattle, WA 98122

Café Nordo:
109 S Main St., Seattle, WA 98104

Carlile Room, The:
820 Pine St., Seattle, WA 98101

Chaco Canyon Organic Café:
8404 Greenwood Ave. N, Seattle, WA 98103

Cheese Wizards:
Roaming food truck

Can Can Culinary Cabaret:
94 Pike St., Seattle, WA 98101

Columbia City Bakery:
4865 Rainier Ave. S, Seattle, WA 98118

Crumpet Shop, The:
1503 First Ave., Seattle, WA 98101

Dick's Drive-In:
115 Broadway E, Seattle, WA 98102

Duke's Seafood & Chowder:
901 Fairview Ave. N, Seattle, WA 98109

Easy Street Records Cafe:
4559 California Ave. SW, Seattle, WA 98116

FareStart:
700 Virginia St., Seattle, WA 98101

Full Tilt Ice Cream:
5041 Rainier Ave. S, Seattle, WA 98118

**Frank's Oyster House &
Champagne Parlor:**
2616 NE Fifty-Fifth St., Seattle, WA 98105

Gainsbourg:
8550 Greenwood Ave. N, Seattle, WA 98103

Hattie's Hat:
5231 Ballard Ave. NW, Seattle, WA 98107

Heaven Sent Fried Chicken:
509 S Third St., Renton, WA 98057

HoneyHole Sandwiches:
703 E Pike St., Seattle, WA 98122

Hotel Albatross:
2319 NW Market St., Seattle, WA 98107

Jack's BBQ:
3924 Airport Way S, Seattle, WA 98108

Jemil's Big Easy:
Roaming food truck

JuneBaby:
2122 NE Sixty-Fifth St., Seattle, WA 98115

Kedai Makan:
1802 Bellevue Ave., Seattle, WA 98122

Kona Kitchen:
8501 Fifth Ave. NE, Seattle, WA 98115

La Carta de Oaxaca:
5431 Ballard Ave. NW, Seattle, WA 98107

La Isla:
2320 NW Market St., Seattle, WA 98107

La Marzocco Café at KEXP:
472 First Ave. N, Seattle, WA 98109

Le Pichet:
1933 First Ave., Seattle, WA 98101

Little Uncle:
1523 E Madison St., #101, Seattle, WA 98122

Lottie's Lounge:
4900 Rainier Ave. S, Seattle, WA 98118

Luc:
2800 E Madison St., Seattle, WA 98112

Lunchbox Laboratory:
1253 Thomas St., Seattle, WA 98109

Marination:
1660 Harvard Ave. SW, Seattle, WA 98126

Matt's in the Market:
94 Pike St., #32, Seattle, WA 98101

Meet the Moon:
120 Lakeside Ave., Seattle, WA 98122

Modernist Cuisine:
14360 SE Eastgate Way, Bellevue, WA 98007

Molly Moon's Ice Cream:
1622.5 N Forty-Fifth St., Seattle, WA 98103

Morsel:
4754 University Way NE, Seattle, WA 98105

Naked City Brewing:
8564 Greenwood Ave. N, Seattle, WA 98103

Napkin Friends:
Roaming food truck

Nue:
1519 Fourteenth Ave., Seattle, WA 98122

Oak:
3019 Beacon Ave. S, Seattle, WA 98144

Oddfellows Cafe + Bar:
1525 Tenth Ave., Seattle, WA 98122

Off the Rez:
Roaming food truck

Oliver's Twist:
6822 Greenwood Ave. N, Seattle, WA 98103

Ooink:
1416 Harvard Ave., Seattle, WA 98122

Pam's Kitchen:
1715 N Forty-Fifth St., Seattle, WA 98103

Patty Pan Grill Cooperative:
15550 Twenty-Seventh Ave. NE, Shoreline, WA 98155

Pecos Pit Bar-B-Que:
2260 First Ave. S, Seattle, WA 98134

Pomodoro:
2366 Eastlake Ave. E, Seattle, WA 98102

Portage Bay Cafe:
391 Terry Ave. N, Seattle, WA 98109

Pink Door, The:
1919 Post Alley, Seattle, WA 98101

Proletariat Pizza:
9622 Sixteenth Ave. SW, Seattle, WA 98106

Ray's Boathouse:
6049 Seaview Ave. NW, Seattle, WA 98107

Revel:
513 Westlake Ave. N, Seattle, WA 98109

Rickshaw, The:
322 N 105th St., Seattle, WA 98133

Roxbury Lanes:
2823 SW Roxbury St., Seattle, WA 98126

Safeco Field:
1250 First Ave. S, Seattle, WA 98134

Salumi Artisan Cured Meats:
309 Third Ave. S, Seattle, WA 98104

Señor Moose:
5242 Leary Ave. NW, Seattle, WA 98107

Serafina (and Cicchetti):
2043 Eastlake Ave. E, Seattle, WA 98102

Shorty's:
2222 Second Ave., Seattle, WA 98121

Sisters and Brothers:
1128 S Albro Pl., Seattle, WA 98108

Skillet Street Food:
1400 E Union St., Seattle, WA 98122

Spinasse:
1531 Fourteenth Ave., Seattle, WA 98122

Station, The:
1600 S Roberto Maestas Festival St., Seattle, WA 98144

Sushi Kappo Tamura:
2968 Eastlake Ave. E, Seattle, WA 98102

Tacos Chukis:
219 Broadway E, Seattle, WA 98102

Tai Tung:
655 S King St., Seattle, WA 98104

Tankard & Tun:
1415 First Ave., Seattle, WA 98101

Taste of India:
5517 Roosevelt Way NE, Seattle, WA 98105

Teachers Lounge, The:
8505 Greenwood Ave. N, Seattle, WA 98103

Top Pot Doughnuts:
609 Summit Ave. E, Seattle, WA 98102

Triple XXX Rootbeer Drive-In:
98 NE Gilman Blvd., Issaquah, WA 98027

Wallyburger:
1719 N Forty-Fifth St., Seattle, WA 98103

Wandering Goose, The:
403 Fifteenth Ave. E, Seattle, WA 98112

Wedgwood Broiler, The:
8230 Thirty-Fifth Ave. NE, Seattle, WA 98115

Westward:
2501 N Northlake Way, Seattle, WA 98103

Whale Wins, The:
3506 Stone Way N, Seattle, WA 98103

XI'AN Noodles:
5259 University Way NE, Seattle, WA 98105

Yoroshiku:
1911 N Forty-Fifth St., Seattle, WA 98103

Zippy's Giant Burgers:
9614 Fourteenth Ave. SW, Seattle, WA 98106